Beside Herself

'Fiercely funny writing . . . desperately watchable'
Claire Armitstead, *Financial Times*

'Sarah Daniels writes crisp dialogue . . . credible and
harrowing. She also provides a myth-debunking prelude
set in a supermarket Hell, where the likes of Lot's Wife,
Jezebel and Delilah bemoan their fate among shelves of
Ritz crackers'
Jim Hiley, *Listener*

Beside Herself premièred at the Royal Court Theatre,
London in March 1990.

Sarah Daniels' plays include **Ripen Our Darkness**
(Royal Court Theatre Upstairs, London, 1981); **Ma's
Flesh Is Grass** (Crucible Studio Theatre, Sheffield, 1981);
The Devil's Gateway (Royal Court Theatre Upstairs,
London, 1983); **Masterpieces** (Manchester Royal
Exchange, 1983; Royal Court Theatre, London, 1983/4);
Neaptide, winner of the 1982 George Devine Award
(Cottesloe, National Theatre, London, 1986); **Byrthrite**
(Royal Court Theatre, London, 1986); **The Gut Girls**
(Albany Empire, Deptford, 1988) and **Beside Herself**
(Royal Court Theatre, London, 1990).

Sarah Daniels

Beside Herself

Methuen Drama

A Methuen Modern Play

First published in 1990 in the Womens Playhouse Plays series as a
Methuen paperback original by Methuen Drama, Michelin House,
81 Fulham Road, London SW3 6RB in association with the
Womens Playhouse Trust, Garden Studios, 11–15 Betterton Street,
London WC2 and distributed in the United States of
America by HEB Inc., 361 Hanover Street, Portsmouth,
New Hampshire NH 03801 3959.

This revised edition published in the Methuen Modern Plays series
in 1991.

Copyright © Sarah Daniels, 1990, 1991

A CIP catalogue record for this book is available from the British
Library.

ISBN 0-413-65910-0

The photograph on the front cover shows Dinah Stabb as Evelyn.
The photograph on the back cover from left to right clockwise shows
June Watson as Mrs Lot, Lizzy McInnerny as Delilah, Dinah Stabb
as Jezebel and Marion Bailey as Eve. Both photos are by Lesley
McIntyre.

Photoset by Rowland Phototypesetting Ltd
Bury St Edmunds, Suffolk.
Printed and bound in Great Britain
by Cox and Wyman Ltd, Reading, Berks.

Caution

Beside Herself premièred at the Royal Court Theatre, London on 29 March 1990 with the following cast:

George/Dave	Tenniel Evans
Evelyn	Dinah Stabb
Eve	Marion Bailey
Shirley/Gaynor	Julia Hills
Lil	June Watson
Teddy	Mark Tandy
Greg/Richard	Nick Dunning
Roy/Tony	Des McAleer
Nicola	Lizzy McInnerny

Members of the cast double in the prelude to the play.

Directed by Jules Wright
Designed by Jenny Tiramani
Lighting by Jenny Cane

The play is set in London in the present.

Prelude

The Power and the Story

A dream. A supermarket.

Delilah *is cutting* **Jezebel**'s *hair.* **Mrs Lot** *is reading a copy of* Family Circle. *She looks up as* **Eve** *approaches.*

Mrs Lot Oh no, that's all we need.

Jezebel Ignore her, then she'll go away.

Delilah You can't do that, Jezebel. Hello, Eve.

Eve How lovely to see you, Delilah.

Delilah This is Jezebel and, er, Lot's wife, sorry I don't know your name.

Mrs Lot Hello, Eve. Where've you bin?

Eve What do you mean, where've I been? I've been here, Hell.

Jezebel (*to* **Mrs Lot**) If we're stuck here, I hardly think Eve would have gone to the other place – use your loaf.

Delilah (*to* **Eve**) Did you want a haircut then?

Eve Not just now, thank you, Delilah. I'm supposed to be taking a tutorial group on 'The burden of guilt and two thousand years of misrepresentation'.

Jezebel Oh Lor, who to?

Eve You, Jezebel, well all of you.

Jezebel Me? I only came over here for a trim.

Eve Only I've been stood on my tod for half a millennium and nobody turned up.

Jezebel Surprise, surprise.

Delilah Most seemed to have opted for Mrs Noah's seminar on 'How to survive a barbecue in a storm'.

Mrs Lot The others are clustered round 'Obedience and

the dire consequences thereof' – to the right of frozen veg. Hey, Delilah, do you think you could make any headway with this frowzy brillo-pad?

Delilah (*examines* **Mrs Lot**'s *hair*) Tut tut, too much conditioning too often. Very bad for your natural body, Lottie love.

Mrs Lot Oh, just chop the lot off, Delilah.

Delilah To tell the truth, I ain't really got the nerve for that any more, lost me bottle. I'll get rid of the split ends if you like.

Eve We spend an eternity condemned to wander these aisles alone and the first chance we get to meet, the only thing you want to highlight is your vanity.

Mrs Lot No need to get all hairiated, Eve. It was her profession. Even if her credibility was undermined before she was fully qualified.

Eve That's what we're here to sort out. How we've –

Jezebel Oh, what's the point. Let sleeping mud puddles lie.

Eve I hardly think you can refer to a series of violent deaths and twenty centuries of trivialisation as a mud puddle, Jezebel.

Jezebel And I don't need you to tell me to what I can or can't refer.

Delilah Keep your hair on. What d'yer want to know, Eve? That I was damned for being an evil castrating bitch. Because that's what everybody believes I am. But do they ever bother to try and imagine what it was like for me being married to a man for whom an afternoon's work was killing a few hundred people with the jaw-bone of a donkey?

Mrs Lot Come on, you must have done something.

Delilah It was his hair, weren't it. To cut a long story short – I did.

Jezebel You didn't ask his permission, did you?

Delilah Don't you start. It really got on his nerves. It come half-way down his bum and it was always getting tangled up in his armpit when he was asleep. He was so strong, see, that if he woke up with a jerk he nearly yanked his own bloody head off. I done him a favour really. Not that you'd know it.

Mrs Lot At least you've got a name. All I'm known as is the wife of Lot, the stupid slag who deserved all she got.

Eve See, that's what we're here to put right.

Mrs Lot Oh, Eve, it weren't that bad really. Na, see we had to abandon our house in a hurry. I only had the shoes I stood up in. Well, when one's home town suffers an arson attack from God, one doesn't exactly dither around pondering on which worldly possessions to pack. So there I was right, running hell for leather, molten brimstone spurting and squirting on my heels when me left shoe got caught in the rubble. So the choice was turn round and retrieve the shoe or hop to the Promised Land. I turned. A mere revolution for which I got metamorphosed into a pillar of salt.

Jezebel That's justice for you.

Mrs Lot Oh, it could be worse. I know people make jokes about 'pass Lot's wife' but they'll get their come-uppance cos I can tell you for a fact salt does for the blood pressure.

Martha *comes over.*

Martha Sorry to bother you. I'm Martha and –

Eve You're in the wrong place, dear. New Testament workshops are over there. (*Pointing.*) Mugs and kitchen tools.

Jezebel And I can still see Mary Mag wandering around the toiletries like a lost sheep.

Eve Probably trying to locate the corn plasters.

Martha For your information I've not had time to sit and listen to everyone's life story, muggins here has had to prepare lunch.

Delilah Oh, I thought Salome was giving you a hand.

Martha She's got a lot on her plate.

Jezebel Just so long as it doesn't end up on ours.

Martha So, how many of you are vegetarians?

Jezebel None.

Eve Speak for yourself.

Delilah Apart from Eve here, who'd die for an Eden Vale yoghurt.

Eve Not one with fruit in, I wouldn't.

Martha So, that's one. Thanks. Sorry for interrupting.

Mrs Lot So useless that Lot.

Jezebel Silly little po-faced domestic.

Mrs Lot I weren't alluding to her, Jezebel. I meant my husband.

Jezebel Ho. You think you had problems. As far as my old man was concerned moral fibre was a brand of breakfast cereal. Weak? You could've knocked him over with a Shredded Wheat.

Eve I wish we could just get on.

Mrs Lot We are, we are. Let's face it, none of us will see two thousand and one again.

Delilah So what happened to you?

Jezebel Me? Dear, I was eaten up by mad dogs.

Mrs Lot Isn't it funny what gets remembered and what gets forgotten.

Delilah Hilarious.

Mrs Lot Because I never did anything when all's said and done. One evening we was all sat down like a happy family, looking forward to a game of Scrabble.

Delilah Don't you mean squabble?

Eve Shush, Delilah, you've had your turn.

Delilah Was that it? Thanks a million.

Mrs Lot Two strangers came to our home. And a mob of pimps and rapists gathered outside demanding access to them. Rather than offend the two guests who Lot had never laid eyes on before, he shouted out of the window to the mob that they could have our daughters instead, using as sales patter, the fact that they were both virgins. This is all totally forgotten. But s'pose Lot had got his own way, I'd have been powerless to stop them.

Delilah Maybe that's why you got turned into a pillar of salt.

Mrs Lot No, that was because I turned back.

Eve At least you did something to be judged for.

Delilah So did you Eve. I mean all credit to you. You climbed the tree of knowledge even if it did fall into your lap in the shape of a manky bit of fruit.

Jezebel I've always meant to ask, was it actually an apple?

Eve No, it was a ripe avocado.

Jezebel Did it taste nice?

Eve Horrible – why d'you think I only took one bite.

Mrs Lot They perk up with a bit of salt.

Eve I caused your downfall and all you care about is a mouldy avocado.

Mrs Lot Don't take on, Eve. We all know you was talked into it.

Eve A red herring.

Jezebel Oh? I always thought it was a serpent. Still, I've never claimed oral history was my strong point.

Eve It was a snake but it didn't talk. Just being. That was my crime. When mankind gets found out he points at me. Her fault – seducer. Made from Adam, for Adam. His wife and his daughter – legitimizer of his will.

Jezebel Listen, we're getting fed up of being harangued by your homilies, Eve.

Delilah Speak for yourself.

Mrs Lot Shush.

They stop, as a **Woman***, pushing a trolley full of shopping, walks between them. She hasn't noticed that her* **Younger Child** *has climbed out of the seat and is now clinging to the side of the trolley. She is more concerned with the whereabouts of the other child,* **Jack***, who is nowhere to be seen.*

Woman (*letting go of the trolley, without looking at* **Younger Child**) Wait there. (*Walks back.*) Jack, where are you? Please, Jack. (*Then sees him clutching bags of crisps.*) Oh, there you are.

She takes the crisps from him, throws them back on the shelves and takes his hand.

You mustn't wander off or I might lose you. No, this way. Now, quickly. Why? Because this isn't a theme park. It's a bloody boring supermarket and we have to get to the post office before lunchtime. Because if we get there too late the queue will be outside the door and we'll get stuck behind someone who wants a stamp of every denomination, an airmail sticker without the rest of the letter and a padded envelope of a size they eventually won't have, by which time I'll be asking for a padded cell. So, please. Come on, take my hand.

Back at the trolley she lets go of **Jack***'s hand to retrieve the* **Younger Child***.* **Jack** *uses the opportunity to grab more crisps.*

You wanted to sit there so sit still. Jack, put those . . . (*Struggle of the crisps ensues.*) Because we can't afford them, that's why. Put them back. Jack? Because they're all full of animal fat – yuck, horrible.

She takes them from him, throws them back on the shelf. **Jack** *throws himself down in front of the trolley.*

Woman Come on, Jack, get up. Please come on. There's no need to make this noise. Don't say I didn't warn you.

Mrs Lot What the bleedin' heaven is she on about?

Jezebel Take no notice, she's lost her trolley.

The **Woman** *pushes the trolley forward.* **Jack** *rolls out of the way and the three of them disappear round the corner.*

Eve Where was I – Oh, yes, if it wasn't for me –

Mrs Lot Can we get back to having our hair cut, Eve. This is getting a bit depressing.

Eve Wait till Lilith gets here. She'll tell you.

Mrs Lot Who?

Eve Adam's first wife who refused to lie beneath him and got the big E.

Jezebel Nobody believes she's anybody. You're crazy.

Eve Oh, am I? I didn't take a bite out of the friggin' forbidden fruit for the good of my health.

Delilah Yeah, I know who she means. Lilith. The one who let us cop for the lot.

Mrs Lot Why do you have to keep dragging his name into it?

Eve Only she got away.

Jezebel She's hardly likely to turn up in here then, is she?

Thunder and lightning.

Man (*VO*) Would those women causing absolute havoc please put a sock in it. Yes, you in the biscuit aisle. Some poor devil has collapsed by fresh fruit and we're holding you resposible.

Mrs Lot Oh, crumbs.

Eve Oh, Christ.

Delilah What's new?

Scene One

In her father's house

George *hears the front door shut. He pours water from the kettle into the teapot.*

Eve *by fridge.*

George (*by table, calls*) Hello?

Evelyn (*calls*) It's only me.

George (*calls*) In here.

Evelyn, *carrying four bags of shopping, comes in. She sees* **Eve** *slouched against a cupboard.*

George *stirs the tea with a spoon, his back to* **Evelyn**.

Evelyn *is visibly shaken by* **Eve**'s *presence. She looks at her. Hesitates. Makes a decision to focus on* **George** *as he turns to face her and puts the teapot on the table.*

George (*laughingly*) You're just on time. (*He sits down.*)

Evelyn Yes, yes. (*Smiling politely.*) I can't stop, I'm very busy.

George (*pouring the tea*) I thought you'd like a cup of tea.

Eve *watches* **George** *and* **Evelyn**. **Evelyn** *is aware of this. She doesn't look at* **Eve**.

Evelyn No. (*Nicely.*) I've already had one thanks, Dad.

She puts the contents of the bag on a work surface where she can see **George**, *but he has to turn round to see her. Throughout the scene she calmly and methodically places each item in the appropriate place, be it cupboard, freezer or fridge.*

Eve Thanks, Dad. Only me. Nobody. Nothing.

George (*pleasantly*) There's no rule about not having another one. Come on. It's getting cold.

Evelyn I've only just had my breakfast.

George Leave that, Evelyn, I can do that when you've gone.

Evelyn The sooner it's done, the better; it's out of the way.

George Sit down for a few minutes. You look quite pale.

Eve *stands*.

Evelyn Oh, I'm fine. Nothing that a good night's sleep won't put right.

George Noises in the house that have always been there take on a loud significance when you're on your own, don't they?

Eve I was never on my own.

Evelyn (*vaguely*) Umm.

George Phillip? Still away?

Evelyn Yes.

George It's very kind of him to always bring you over with the shopping but it's also nice to see you on your own for once.

Eve *smirks*.

Evelyn It's quite a trek though.

George And I really do appreciate it. How's things otherwise?

Evelyn Oh, you know, busy.

George Keeping busy is the wicket keeper of coping, that I do know.

Eve *mimes lifting a cricket bat in the air*.

George We had so many plans your mother and I for when I retired. But, now, well, it's not the same when you're on your own.

Evelyn (*goes to fridge*) No.

Eve *follows her and stands behind her.*

George (*jovially*) Evelyn, will you please stop fussing.

Evelyn (*putting things in the fridge*) It's no good leaving things uncovered in there, they just rot.

Eve *laughs softly*.

George Oh, I'll have a clear out when you've gone. (*Cajolingly.*) Please sit down, how am I supposed to talk to you when you've got your head in the ruddy fridge.

Evelyn The microwavable dinners are arranged in order of their sell-by date. And, oh, you've still got some left . . .

George I still get invited out from time to time, dinner parties and do's of one sort or another. Besides, I don't like a lot of that goo under ruptured cellophane.

Evelyn Why didn't you tell me? (*Turns to face him.*) What do you like, and I'll make sure I get it next time?

Eve *kicks the fridge*.

Eve *walks away from* **Evelyn**, *stands back but between* **Evelyn** *and* **George**.

George What I'd really like is for you to sit down and talk to me.

Evelyn (*continues with putting the shopping away*) It's just that I have a meeting to go to and I'm running a bit late.

George I was going to suggest that you might like to come with me to one of these do's and what not. I'm often asked to bring a guest. It would do you good, to get out in the evenings with Phillip away so often. After all, what's good for the gander is good for the goose.

Evelyn (*unguarded*) What do you mean by that?

Eve You're thick.

George Nothing. Just that/

Evelyn What?

George If he's out enjoying himself I don't see why/

Evelyn You know I want to finish redecorating the house and with my daytimes rather full . . .

George (*sympathetically*) You take on too much, Evelyn. Being the wife of an MP doesn't mean you have to spend every waking hour in voluntary work.

Evelyn It's important to practise what you preach.

George And charity begins at home.

Evelyn (*indignant*) Dad, I do your shopping every fortnight. (*Goes to the cupboard and puts the tins away.*)

George (*hurt rather than angry*) I don't care about the shopping. I'd prefer a bit more of your company.

Evelyn I know.

George I'm not asking much.

Eve (*sarcastic*) You've never given much.

George We never asked much. When your mother was alive we hardly ever saw you. Now it's just me and you.

Eve (*sneers*) It's the least you can do.

George It's just putting the poor old man's shopping away with a 'yes', 'no', 'thank you for asking' and you're off. (*Turning round angry.*) For God's sake, Evelyn. Look at me when I'm talking to you.

He stands suddenly, accidentally knocking his cup and saucer on the floor. They smash. The noise makes **Evelyn** *and* **Eve** *jump in fright.*

Eve *covers her face and drops to the floor.*

George (*pathetically*) Damn! Damn!

Evelyn (*shakily*) It's all right. It was only an accident. No real damage done.

George (*sits down again, miserably*) Oh, God. I can't bear getting old.

Eve Then drop dead.

Evelyn (*shocked, responds to* **Eve***)* I'm sorry, I didn't mean that.

George What?

Evelyn To make you angry.

George (*apologetically*) I didn't mean to lose my temper –
it's the last thing (*He reaches out to put his hand reassuringly on
hers. She avoids him.*) I wanted to happen.

Evelyn (*picking up the broken china*) Don't worry, I'll get
you a replacement next time I'm in town. (*She goes over to
the bin and throws it away.*)

George (*sighs*) God knows I don't want to turn into one of
those pathetic old goats who constantly makes demands on
his family. What with your brothers so far away, it would
be nice to see you and Phillip and Joanna a bit more often.

Evelyn (*lamely*) We always spend Christmas.

George But darling, Christmas.

Evelyn Yes, I know it was months ago. But, you know,
Phillip has a lot on and with Joanna away at school . . .

George I got a letter from her the other day.

Eve and **Evelyn** *are both unnerved.*

Eve *is closer to* **Evelyn** *at this point than at any other point in the
scene.*

Evelyn (*coldly*) She didn't mention it.

George Thanking me for her birthday present. At least
she keeps in touch. Many youngsters of her age can't be
bothered to sit down and write a word unless it's to scrawl
doggerel over tube train doors. It was a really chatty,
almost witty piece of prose. She's really quite intelligent,
you know. I've often wondered if we should have paid for
your education. But at the time . . . Still, Joanna's a real
credit to you.

Evelyn Which is more than you can say of me.

Eve Dunce.

George Oh, come on. I'm very proud of you, you know
that.

Evelyn (*surprised*) Are you?

Eve (*jeers*) You're pathetic.

George Yes, of course.

Eve *moves away in disgust.*

Joanna said that she'd come and see me in the summer holidays.

Eve *turns back. Her concentration now strongly focused on* **George**.

Evelyn She can't. Not on her own.

George Nonsense.

Evelyn She's not old enough.

George She's old enough to get on the tube.

Evelyn It's too far.

George I'd meet her at the station.

Evelyn No. (*Then.*) I'll bring her over.

George Would you? That would be nice. Thank you.

Evelyn (*hurriedly*) And I'll see you in a fortnight. I must dash now. Sorry, I really do have to go. Sorry. 'Bye.

Evelyn *walks towards the door.* **Eve** *follows her.*

Eve (*jeeringly*) Sorry, sorry, sorry.

Evelyn (*turns*) 'Bye.

Eve Sorry.

Scene Two

St Dymphna's

The living room of a Community Group Home.

Along the back wall is a door which leads to a walk-in cupboard. To the left a door which leads to the rest of the house. To the right a door which leads to the hallway and front door.

The room has been vandalised. The recently emulsioned walls have been daubed with paint. The only decipherable word 'Loonies' has pride of place between the picture rail and frame of the mirror over the fireplace. The mirror is smashed. The fragments lie scattered over the floor.

Lil *enters. She carries a shopping bag containing cleaning materials and her overall. She puts the bag down and surveys the room with pragmatic dismay.*

Shirley (*VO from the cupboard*) Is that you, Lil?

Lil (*looks round*) Shirley? Where are you?

Shirley (*VO*) Won't be a sec. I'm just getting changed for the meeting.

Lil *puts bag by fireplace.*

Teddy, *complete with dog collar, enters right.*

Teddy (*blithely*) Front door open. Sorry. Shirley about?

Lil (*whirls round. Anxious to protect* **Shirley** *from being caught in a state of undress by a clergyman*) Cup of tea, Father? (*Turning back momentarily to check the cupboard door is still shut.*)

Teddy (*magnanimously*) Oh, Teddy, please.

Lil (*distractedly*) Eh? Oh, you want the Day Centre. They do a nice line in soft toys.

Teddy (*perturbed. Calls out*) Shirley?

Shirley (*VO from cupboard*) Coming.

Shirley *emerges smartly dressed. Track suit over her arm.*

Teddy Ah, there you are.

Shirley Good morning, Teddy. You're nice and early. (*She watches him as he looks at the state of the room.*) Not a pretty picture. I've made a start in the kitchen, Lil.

Teddy Were you here when it happened?

Shirley No. Oh, I'm so sorry, you've not been introduced. Lil, this is the Reverend Kegwin.

Teddy Teddy. I've recently been co-opted on to the

Management Committee. (*Holds out his hand.*) Pleased to meet you, Lil.

Lil (*letting him shake her hand robustly*) How d'you do.

Pause.

Teddy (*brightly*) Where are the other residents?

Shirley (*short embarrassed laugh*) Oh, Lil isn't a resident. She works for the Local Authority. Twelve of her working hours a week are allotted to us here at St Dymphna's.

Teddy Mea culpa. Mea culpa. You're a Home Help.

Lil In a glorified manner of speaking. I actually work for the EDT.

Shirley (*in response to* **Teddy**'s *bewildered look*) The Early Discharge Team – to support those recently discharged from psychiatric hospitals into Group Homes like this – by way of daily living skills.

Lil Yeah, we used to be called 'Aides' but that word don't exactly inspire confidence in the public imagination. (*She starts to tidy the room.*)

Teddy Umm 'discharge' doesn't exactly roll off the tongue either. (*Then jollying up.*) Still, I expect you're an old hand at this now.

Slight pause.

Shirley (*quickly*) I've made a list of the items missing and the damage. It's –

Teddy You know my feeling is that we should have a plaque or something on the outside with 'St Dymphna's' embossed on it.

Shirley (*mildly*) Would that do any good? I mean do churches named after saints get less vandalised than ones that aren't?

Teddy (*vaguely*) No idea. I've never thought about it. (*Then enthusiastically.*) But. I've been mugging up on St Dymphna.

Shirley (*smiling*) Oh, Teddy, I didn't know you had ecumenical tendencies.

Teddy (*seriously*) Only towards Anglo-Catholicism I hasten to reassure you. My views on Evangelical   · Liberalism are, I imagine, akin to the Romanian layman's on Stalin.

Shirley (*unreassured*) I see, (*Gestures towards the door.*) I've just got to . . .

Teddy (*he follows her towards the door. Then stops. Looks at the graffiti*) Remarkable. Seems like Community Mental Health is popular with everybody except the community. One thing's for sure, if I were psychologically disturbed I wouldn't want to sit and stare at the word 'Loonies' all day.

Shirley Yes, no, me neither. I don't know how we're going to manage to get them repainted.

Teddy The insurance?

Shirley These things take time.

Teddy No time like the present. Where did you say the details were?

Shirley On my desk.

Teddy Why don't I go and give them the once over and get on the blower to the insurance company?

He goes.

Shirley *sighs. Shakes her head.*

Lil *kneels on the floor and picks up the broken pieces of mirror.*

Shirley (*to* **Lil**) Remind me to order a new mirror. (*She bends down to help* **Lil**.)

Lil (*holding a piece of mirror*) Unnerving, ain't it – how you can only see a piece of yourself in a shard of mirror. It's sort of like trying to recollect a dream when you can only visualise the bit that woke you up.

Shirley (*not knowing what to say*) Oh?

Lil (*smiles*) I don't know what come over me. I must have read it in a book.

Shirley Are you a big reader then?

Lil Never used to be. Just took it up to pass the time. Now that, well now that I have more time.

Shirley How is your husband?

Lil Oh, he's home. They're all very pleased with him.

Shirley I don't imagine you get much time for reading at the moment or does your daughter help out?

Lil My . . .

Shirley You do have a daughter, or am I mixing you up with someone else? No, I'm sure . . .

Lil Yes, yes, but it's difficult. She's away a lot.

Shirley What does she do?

Lil (*hasn't seen her daughter for eight years and has no idea what she does. Lies.*) She's er, an air hostess.

Shirley Really? Does . . .

Lil I get postcards from all over the place. Well, this won't buy the baby new shoes. I'd better get the Hoover. There is still a Hoover?

Shirley I forgot to check. If we haven't it's not on his list.

As they go towards the door left, conscious of the awkwardness, **Lil** *changes the subject.*

Lil Fancy calling something in a dog collar Teddy. I ask you. Jesus. (*Then.*) You know I thought this place was called 77 Headsend Road. That's what it says on my work sheet. Who the hell is St Dymphna when she's at home?

Shirley (*smiles*) Don't look at me, the funding body christened it.

Lil (*snorts*) Wretched Voluntary Sector. Cluttered with born-agains.

Shirley I better go and see what he's doing.

Lil Well at least he put his frock on before he got here.

They go out.

Evelyn *comes in. She carries a framed print of Breughel's* Icarus.

Evelyn I knew it was supposed to be unlucky to have a mirror over a fireplace but – (*Pause.*) I look good.

Eve Stupid.

Evelyn (*to* **Eve**) I feel okay.

Eve Dirty.

Evelyn (to **Eve**) I'm all right.

Eve Worthless.

Evelyn Now, best place for the picture.

Eve You shouldn't talk to yourself. Not here of all places.

Evelyn (*holding the picture against the wall*) No.

Lil *comes in with the vacuum cleaner.*

Lil (*flatly*) Talking to yourself, Evelyn?

Evelyn (*coldly*) Merely reflecting on my sanity out loud, Lil.

Lil Oh, really?

Evelyn Yes, haven't you heard that expression?

Lil No. What is it? Ascot blank verse?

Evelyn I brought this. I thought it might disguise some of the mess until you've had time to clean up.

Lil That's nice.

Evelyn Oh, it's not mine. I borrowed it from the library. Not the one round here. That's closed. Crying shame and in a Labour borough.

Lil *sighs audibly and switches on the vacuum cleaner.*

Pause.

Lil *vacuums round the fireplace.*

Evelyn (*shouts over the noise of the vacuum cleaner*) Shall I hang it over the fireplace?

Lil (*switches the vacuum cleaner off*) Why not? (*She gets a cloth and a bottle of white spirit from her bag.*)

Evelyn *stands on a chair, takes a picture hook from her pocket and hangs the picture so that it neatly covers the word 'Loonies'.*

Eve She's laughing at you.

Lil *isn't taking any notice. She concentrates on removing the paint that's been daubed on the fire surround.*

Evelyn *steps down and puts the chair back.*

Shirley *enters left, unseen by* **Lil** *or* **Evelyn**.

Evelyn (*looking at the picture*) There. (*Pompously.*) I know some people don't like Breughel but then some people do.

Lil (*casually without looking up*) And, there's every probability his wife painted it anyway.

Evelyn (*curtly*) Really? (*Slight pause.*) He wasn't a homosexual then.

Shirley What a cost-effective idea.

Evelyn Thank you. Though I don't imagine that even the Tate has got enough stock to cover this doggerel.

Eve One of Daddy's words.

Shirley The? Oh, yes, the graffiti. It's not just this room. Teddy's upstairs now trying to evaluate the extent of the damage.

Evelyn Bless him. I'd better follow suit if I'm going to be in the picture for this meeting.

She goes.

Shirley Did his wife really paint it?

Lil (*still working*) No idea. I just said it.

Shirley Oh, d'you think he was gay then?

Lil (*lightly*) I really don't know. I suppose it's possible. Most talented people seem to have been. (*Starts to rub at the* *paint with a vengeance*.) Typical of her to try and get one over on me like that. (*Calmer*.) It was all because of her I took up reading in the first place.

Shirley Of her?

Lil Yeah. Them sort. All the same. Always casually relating real life to make-believe. To show off their education.

Shirley How do you mean?

Lil Oh, you know, something ordinary happens, some trivial everyday occurrence and they'll pipe up (*Mimicking*.) 'Oh, that's so reminiscent of so and so when that happens in that book so and so . . .'

Shirley Which book?

Lil Could be anything, who knows. The usual trick is to refer to a character and not the book's title. So if you ain't read the right book you're all at sea and if you have you have to be thinking on your feet.

Shirley Oh, I see what you mean. I always feel sorry for them not being able to relate anything to real life.

Lil Pah, I keep running up against her. I tell yer, Shirley, she's sat on more committees that I have buses. And she's always looked down her nose at me right from the time I used to clean for the old people in Swans' Walk.

Shirley She doesn't strike me as the sort of woman to be conversing chapter and verse with the cleaner.

Lil (*excited*) That's just it, Shirley. I had her down as one of them types but I'm telling yer she don't know the difference between a Trollope and a Tolstoy. All I can think is she must have spent all her time at school reading *Wish for a Pony* under the desk.

Shirley You've ploughed through loads of classics for her benefit to find she hasn't read one of them?

Lil (*laughs*) Yeah. (*She stands, wipes over the fire surround*.) Aw, don't look at me like that. I don't bother to try and catch her out no more. I do it for meself now. Oh, hark at me, I don't know what I'm going on about, take no notice.

Shirley What sort of books?

Lil Stories. You know. Fiction. The sort you can be absorbed in knowing the only responsibility you've got is to turn the page and it will all be resolved.

Shirley You only read novels with happy endings?

Lil Oh, no. Take Thomas Hardy for instance. He's so depressing that when the main character dies it's a relief to know they've been put out of their misery.

Greg *enters right.* **Greg** *is the Acting Team Leader in the hospital Psychiatric Social Work Department.*

Greg Morning, Lil, Shirley. How's things?

Shirley (*looking at the room*) Could be better.

Lil It'll be clean by the time I'm finished here today. Apart from the writing on the walls, I don't know what to do about that.

Greg (*looking through his papers in his bag*) I'm sure we'll be able to sort something out. I hope. I must say it was good of you to offer us coffee and sandwiches for lunch, Lil.

Lil (*unseen by* **Shirley** *or* **Greg**, *looks quite shocked this being the first time she's heard of it*) Oh. Right. Fine. I'd better go out and get some bread.

Greg Where is everybody?

Shirley The charity cases are still upstairs marvelling over how the actual plumbing got actually nicked.

Greg (*looks up*) Now, Shirley.

Shirley They can't hear us.

Greg Still. Teddy's redeemable, isn't he? He's a bit of a liberal at heart.

Shirley I hope so. He's supposed to be shouldering some of my work balancing the books. (*Sighs.*) When I first started work, I never thought about money. I mean not the responsibility to find money to make the thing work.

Greg I find myself increasingly thinking about money, in respect of how little I get paid, weighed against mounting responsibility, crumbling resources and negligible job satisfaction.

Shirley That good?

Greg (*wearily*) Twenty-three unallocated cases, twelve case conferences so far this month, and to top it all, my motor got pranged in the rear. Moan. Moan. Some well-oiled nut behind the wheel. Cops. (*Apologetically.*) Sorry. There's another euphemism for your research. (*Impatiently.*) Where the bloody hell is Roy?

Shirley Do you call him Roy to his face?

Greg Only when I feel supremely confident. Usually I feel the weight of his status bearing down compelling me to address him as Dr Freeman. Ideally, I try to manage to converse with him without bringing his name into the conversation at all.

Shirley It will be interesting to see how you introduce him – what's he really like?

Greg Heavy drugs merchant. He views psychotherapy with the disdain most men reserve for male ballet dancers. You know that breed of psychiatrist whose only recollection from childhood is some distant memory of a grandfather clock ticking in a great aunt's house. On balance they aren't too keen to examine others' early experiences in case it triggers off some long forgotten trauma in their own past. (*Then.*) Don't mind me, I've just come back from a course in 'Burn Out' – I reckon I've caught it.

Evelyn/Eve and **Teddy** *enter left as* **Roy**, *followed by* **Nicola**, *enters right.*

Greg (*hurriedly mouths to* **Shirley**) Did he hear me?

Shirley *shakes her head.*

Roy A quick start, Greg, please.

Greg Okay.

Roy Hello, Evelyn.

Evelyn Hello, Roy.

Greg Please take a seat, everyone. I'd like to thank you all for being able to get here at such short notice. I know we're running to tight schedules and meeting in our lunch hour. However, we will be provided with a sandwich and coffee shortly. I'd like to welcome the Reverend Teddy Kegwin officially to our Management Committee. I think we all know each other. (*Then seeing* **Nicola**.) Oh, I'm sorry, I don't . . .

Roy (*offhand*) Oh, this is Nurse Cretsley.

Nicola (*self-consciously*) Adams.

Roy (*without a hint of apology*) Nurse sorry Adams, is training to be a CPN, temporarily on placement with me. She's here as an observer. Good experience. She comes from that Godforsaken place.

Nicola Cretsley. And it's Nicola.

Evelyn Hello, I'm Evelyn.

Eve Hello, I'm Evelyn.

Shirley (*writing, looks up*) Sorry, it's just for the minutes. It's not Nicola Cretsley, is it? It's Adams.

Nicola Yes. No. Cretsley's where I've been working.

Shirley (*writing*) I thought so. Thanks. (*Looks up.*) Oh, that's a coincidence. (*Stops herself, then more formally.*) I'm Shirley, by the way. House Manager. Part-time. Because the post is funded part-time.

Roy (*sighs*) This isn't a full blown case conference. It's an emergency ad hoc allocation meeting. Do we need bother with minutes?

Shirley Not formally, no. But it's always useful to have a record.

Greg (*to* **Nicola**) Teddy and Evelyn are part of the

Management Committee and we have a worker from the
EDT for a total of, umm . . .

Teddy Twelve hours a week.

Greg Yes, sorry, my brain's not in gear. Thank you,
Teddy. Oh, and I'm Greg, acting Team Manager for the
Psychiatric Social Work team based in the hospital. So, if
we bump into each other in the corridors we'll know who
we are.

Nicola (*self-consciously*) Hello, hello, hello.

Teddy I think I'm supposed to ask which budget lunch is
coming out of.

Greg We'll get to the budget soon enough, Teddy. First,
any smokers?

Nicola, *rather embarrassed, raises her hand.*

Teddy Tut, tut, a nurse as well.

Evelyn I've given up.

Shirley I didn't know you smoked.

Evelyn Only socially, but I've stopped altogether.

Roy *puts his pen down on his file impatiently.*

Evelyn Now.

Greg (*gathering pace*) Fine, fine. Well, the rule is only one
cigarette to be smoked at a time. (*To* **Nicola**.) So, as long
as you don't put two in your mouth at once you're
laughing. Shirley, would you like to summarise the events
of last week?

Roy We all know what happened last week. It's next week
I'm concerned about.

Shirley It's just that . . .

Roy It's just that I've got wards due to close which are
still chock-a-block. This home has six beds, only four of
which are useable at the present time which represents
approximately four per cent of patients already waiting to
be rehabilitated into the community. And, although these

places are supposed to be half-way hostels, as we all know the turnover is very slow because of the housing situation. They are also, (*Sarcastically*.) for the record, supposed to offer an alternative to the dreaded Victorian asylum. But, what sort of asylum they offer when they get vandalised every other week, I don't know.

Shirley It's only been vandalised once before.

Roy It's only been open six months.

Teddy (*consolingly to* **Shirley**) At least I managed to pin the insurance rep down.

Evelyn Is that why there are so many ill-looking people begging on the underground?

Roy No, it's because we don't have the resources to start with, but let's not allow ourselves to get side-tracked.

Greg I would just like to point out, that because child protection is very much in the public eye, it demands, and rightly, more and more time and necessary statutory work, but its very urgency relegates the support given to those recovering from mental illness, who are out of the picture as far as the public eye and sympathy are concerned, to the bottom of the priority pile.

Roy Now we've all aired our sociological grievances, perhaps you could enlighten me to the relevance, if any, of what you're saying.

Greg Bluntly, that new residents we take on must be those most able to cope, because in person-hours alone, the support is just not available.

Shirley I agree and I would also like it minuted that we do have an Equal Opps policy and should be mindful of that. Also, when things get back to normal, residents should have a say in who lives here.

Teddy As you've got the pen I think you're at liberty to write anything you like.

This uncalled for interruption is coldly ignored.

Sorry.

Roy This EOP rigmarole is all very well except the majority of those needing places are men. Quite incongruous really because statistics show many more women suffer from mental illness.

Shirley That's another thing. The women in this place end up skivvying for the chaps. I mean, very little is done to challenge traditional roles and values.

Greg Yes, well, a lot of men we're trying to place have had nervous breakdowns after their mothers, wives or girlfriends have left them or died and they just can't cope.

Teddy Forgive me, but I can't see anything wrong with that, surely the family is something to aspire to not challenge – isn't that the whole purpose of this project – to create a happy family home as opposed to an institutionalised regime.

Shirley For an awful lot of people 'happy', 'home' and 'family' are not synonyms.

Evelyn If home is where the heart is, I'd live in John Lewis.

Greg Point taken, Shirley.

Teddy (*to* **Shirley**) I would like to take issue with you there.

Roy (*labouredly*) I am concerned with emptying beds, getting people out of hospital and well again and preferably not left to their own devices under railway arches.

Evelyn Surely, none of us want to see anyone on the streets.

Teddy Absolutely.

Greg Eric and Steve will be returning. They're both understandably apprehensive but both expressed a wish to come back.

Roy Would it be possible for some effort to be made to stop them returning to the hospital so much?

Shirley It's been their home, they feel secure there. Besides the canteen food is reasonably cheap.

Greg I was trying to explain earlier, er, Dr Freeman, about how hard pressed we were for putting in that sort of support. Besides, even if we could, it's not our job to police people like that.

Roy I thought that was part of the Management Committee's volunteer role.

Teddy Oh, righto.

Evelyn Yes.

Eve Policing people?

Shirley Steve has actually found a job at the market and Eric will hopefully get a place on a rehabilitation work skills course.

Greg (*to* **Roy**) Mary, I understand, is not yet ready to be discharged in the near future.

Roy No.

Evelyn All this must really have taken its toll.

Roy Yes.

Greg That leaves us with two spaces. When the radiator, wash basin and carpet are restored in the top room, we'll have two more.

Teddy But who knows when that will be.

Greg I have selected a few applicants from a considerable pile, two of whom we must choose. Would you like to talk about them Dr Freeman, or shall I?

Roy Carry on.

Greg (*referring to his notes*) Rohima is twenty. She had a nervous breakdown during the first year at university and had to abandon the course. She was re-admitted to hospital six months after discharge following a suicide attempt. She returned to her bedsit and was re-admitted to hospital after being evicted owing to her refusal to claim

DSS. She is depressed and can still be withdrawn and uncommunicative. However, she has not made any subsequent attempts to take her life.

Roy Everything is exacerbated by her refusal to take the prescribed medication. However, living in some kind of supportive set-up will undoubtedly be beneficial. She needs jollying along a bit and certainly does not warrant a place in hospital. It all seems very straightforward. Can we have a nod of assent on this one?

Greg (*looks round*) Any questions?

Roy No.

Evelyn I was just going to say. No, it's all right.

Greg Fine, good. That's Rohima settled. (*Picking next application.*) Dawn is twenty-two. She has a very severe hearing loss. Her speech is indistinct, often incoherent. She relies heavily on lip reading and doesn't mix with deaf people who use sign language. Because of her lack of communication skills, she finds it difficult to make friends and is very isolated. Five years ago, her child, then aged three months, was taken into care.

Shirley What were you going to say, Evelyn?

Evelyn It doesn't matter. Only that she will have to claim benefit while she's here. No one can expect to live rent free.

Teddy Quite right.

Greg Yes, they all do. (*To* **Roy**.) So far, I think I'm correct in saying she has been difficult to diagnose.

Roy Who are we talking about now?

Greg Dawn.

Roy Yes, yes, she has a personality disorder certainly. It's difficult to tell if she has learning difficulties or if it's the hearing loss.

Shirley Not being able to hear doesn't impair one's brain.

Roy In this game people's prognoses are supposed to be

arrived at after talking to them. If you can't understand what they say, it does complicate things somewhat.

Shirley So she could be talking perfectly rationally. Just that others aren't tuned in to the enunciation.

Roy That's what I said.

Evelyn Suppose someone's so depressed they don't talk at all?

Roy I have a foolproof method, Evelyn, for spotting depression, in women at least. If it gets past four o'clock in the afternoon on the day they're admitted and they still haven't asked for a cup of tea – they're depressed.

Teddy (*laughs*) Oh, that's good. (*Stops, aware that this isn't appropriate behaviour.*)

Evelyn Suppose they don't like tea. (*Pause.*) I know I don't very much.

Greg (*anxious to continue*) Anyway, from time to time Dawn appears in the Self-Harm Unit. She has a history of violent outbursts and has not come to terms with the baby's adoption.

Evelyn Why was the baby adopted?

Greg Oh, that's rather a sad story which I hasten to add I wasn't involved in.

Roy And one we don't need to hear right now, with due respect, Evelyn. Dawn is on medication which has put a stop to the violent outbursts.

Evelyn Roy, we are supposed to be actively involved with the residents' welfare. It does help –

Roy Very well, but a potted precis please, Greg.

Greg (*condensing as he talks*) Dawn ran away from home when she got pregnant. Got a flat and was living alone with the baby. She went out leaving the baby alone. The police got involved when the baby was admitted to hospital with bad burns. Dawn was charged with negligence, put on probation and the baby was taken into care.

Teddy Oh, that's sad.

Greg However, the real story has since emerged. The baby became ill one evening. Dawn wrapped it in a blanket and left it in front of the fire for warmth while she went out to try and persuade someone to 'phone the doctor for her. When she came back the edge of the blanket had caught alight. From then on it seems the system became 'deaf' to the truth.

Teddy Shame.

Greg (*to* **Teddy**) Yes, it is. But, the only effective work that can be done now is trying to get her to accept it.

Roy Adoption is irreversible and she didn't help matters much by physically attacking her Probation Officer. Doesn't like men. Apparently she was sexually messed about with as a child.

Eve You started this. Don't just look out the window.

Nicola (*deep breath*) Actually, I do think it's important –

Greg To be fair, I think it was more that the Probation Officer had rather a profusion of beard and was quite impossible to lip read, although, it is suspected that the father of the child could have been her own father.

Eve Let's go. Come on. Who wants to hear all this?

Nicola I was just about –

Roy (*to* **Greg**) Have you got Dave's application there?

Greg (*surprised*) Yes.

Roy Well, do you think we could move on to it. He has been waiting rather a long while and I was hoping we'd cover him first.

Nicola *takes out a cigarette and lights it.*

Greg Oh, I'm sorry.

Roy Perhaps we could do that now?

Greg As you wish. (*He puts* **Dawn**'s *application down and picks up* **Dave**'s.) Dave is an intelligent man. He's fifty-four and been in institutions for years. Consequently his physical health has suffered. Twenty odd years ago he was sent to Broadmoor when . . .

Teddy (*before he can stop himself*) Broadmoor??!!

Nicola *conscious of everyone's disapproval of the smoke, stubs the cigarette out.*

Roy (*drearily*) It was policy to send a quota of non-criminal patients there in the late sixties to eradicate the stigma of the name. Unfortunately, it had the opposite effect, taking Dave and many others with it.

Evelyn Poor man.

Shirley They'd have done better to change the name like they did with Sellafield. By the time people remember it used to be called Windscale they've forgotten to remember why it was changed.

Greg He has no history of violence to himself or others.

Roy Although when deluded he believes he did kill his father.

Eve With a look? With a word? With a wish? With a thought?

Greg (*flicking through the notes*) Throughout the years no diagnoses seem to have escaped him but (*Looking at the top page. Reading.*) at the beginning of this year, he is schizophrenic and stability is maintained with Modecate. (*Turns over.*) Oh, I see you've put homosexual under diagnosis.

Roy (*flatly*) Well, he is.

Greg (*very politely*) With all respect Dr Freeman, as you know better than me, homosexuality was removed from the ICD-9 over twenty years ago.

Roy (*blithely*) Oh, cross it off then.

Teddy (*unable to completely conceal his panic*) But I take it he has had a test?

Greg (*to* **Roy**) It's just that he might not want everyone to know.

Roy (*to* **Teddy** *mildly*) He's been in an institution for twenty years man. (*To* **Greg**.) Well, it's you who told everybody not me.

Teddy Still, hold on. You can't put people at risk. Don't you agree Evelyn?

Eve Just smile.

Greg I hope I don't need to remind everybody that this meeting is confidential.

Roy (*firmly*) So are my notes.

Teddy Evelyn and I are rather worried. Am I speaking out of turn Evelyn?

Evelyn No, I'm quite all right. Thanks for asking.

Roy I think Dave fits the bill exactly. Time methinks for the promised cup of coffee. (*He looks at* **Shirley**.)

Shirley Refreshment, I assure you, is on its way. However, I would like to point out that if we leave it at that, we'll have three male residents and one female. As the second applicant is a woman I would like to reconsider her application.

Evelyn I thought it was settled.

Roy It's quite preposterous to suggest we start juggling with age, sex, class and race now. I for one am too busy.

Eve Run now.

Greg Shirley does have a point Dr Freeman.

Teddy (*grasping at straws*) And, maybe a 'she' will be more suitable. I mean who are we to set Dawn asunder. Given of course Shirley's criteria. (*Quickly.*) Where does she come from?

Eve You could try and say you've got to go.

Greg (*trying to read the written notes*) Shropshire would it be?

Teddy Ah.

Greg (*peering closely at the paper*) No could be Southshield or Stratford. I can't make it out.

Nicola (*to* **Teddy**) Excuse me but what's so relevant about where she comes from?

Teddy Well, it's a well-known supposedly regular occurrence in some rural pockets – incest, that is. Not to me – to us. Our values. But isn't that what tolerance is all about – not imposing our own brand of morals?

Shirley Isn't that what the church is there for though?

Eve Think of something else.

Teddy For example . . .

Eve Don't think about it.

Teddy I have recently been enlightened about the impact of the imposition of Anglican missionaries on other countries' modus vivendi.

Greg I agree with Nicola. It's not an activity confined by geography or social class Teddy. (*To* **Nicola**.) That is what you were driving at I take it?

Roy (*before* **Nicola** *can reply*) That's not my experience.

Greg Could be because middle class crises don't often cross our path on the NHS these days.

Eve The bathroom. Think about re-decorating the bathroom.

Nicola (*quickly/nervously*) But, statistics show, don't they that a large proportion of female patients in mental institutions were sexually abused by a father figure?

Eve It has got dirty, filthy.

Roy (*scoffs*) I can't imagine where you got that so-called statistic from. (*Then severely*.) And it's not very helpful to use the term 'mental institution' in this day and age.

Eve Pink. Paint it pink?

Greg (*courteously to* **Nicola**) I think it's misleading and potentially dangerous to suggest that abused girls end up as women on psychiatric wards.

Nicola (*quickly*) But I weren't saying –

Roy (*patronisingly*) 'Weren't' you now.

Nicola No, it's a small per cent admitted to hospital, it would have to be. There isn't room for a quarter of the female population.

Roy (*scoffs*) In all my years of experience I could count on one hand the number of patients who've admitted that to me. And they were naughty precocious girls who certainly had no doubts about their attractiveness to men.

Eve Count on one hand. Dirty white, blue grey . . . blue grey . . . blue grey . . .

Greg We do have to be careful in the present climate not to make unfounded or rash judgements based on partial information.

Nicola I do know.

Eve Try and remember the names of the pencils in the box. Ivory, black, gunmetal, terracotta.

Nicola GP's have always pleaded ignorance. Now with the present backlash their ability to avoid the fact is frightening. Without medical evidence no one is believed. They come up with the most unlikely explanations rather than put their necks on the line. Their ability to avoid the facts unless haemorrhaging is actually occurring is frightening.

Eve Count on the other hand. Copper beech, golden brown, raw sienna.

Roy (*cross*) That is grossly inaccurate. If not libellous. You are speaking out of turn Nurse. You are here as an observer.

Eve Olive green, cedar green.

Greg (*wanting to take the heat out of the situation*) What would you put the figure at Shirley? (*To the others.*) Shirley's done quite a lot of research into mental illness for her M Phil.

Shirley Not really. I mean I am doing an M Phil but on how our language is obsessed by turning everything into a noun. Naming it thereby distancing it from personal experience, er, making it safe – er, well, er, there's a chapter on labelling and social behaviour but that's about it.

Greg It's not an original idea you know.

Shirley Of course it's not. If it was, my thesis wouldn't have a bibliography and I wouldn't pass.

Roy Goodo. So you can all feel sorry for me – labelled psychiatrist and subject to all the jokes that go with it. Is that what you mean?

Shirley Yes, no, sort of.

Roy Well is it or isn't it?

Shirley Not really, although I do take your point it's very valid. I . . .

Nicola (*helping her out*) Do you mean loaded words like 'precocious'?

Eve Again. Cedar green, may green, grass green, emerald green.

Shirley Yes, no, sort of.

Roy For your information Nurse 'precocious' is not a noun. I was merely pointing out that adult women I'd/

Nicola (*very unconfidently*) I know Dr Freeman. It's just that, I'd been told that psychiatrists see the adult as the product of the child not the other way round.

Greg 'Product' now that's an interesting word for you Shirley.

Eve Mineral green, jade green, kingfisher blue.

Teddy Nouns by their nature often necessitate gender – boy, girl, husband, wife, mother, daughter/

Roy And where was Dawn's mother in all this. Two safe bets, either gadding about relinquishing her responsibilities or turning a blind eye.

Nicola *lights another cigarette.*

Eve Prussian blue, spectrum blue, ultramarine.

Greg (*consulting notes*) We don't know.

Roy Quite. Besides, it can often be a complex liaison of some duration, indicative of a caring relationship. (*To* **Nicola** *coldly.*) Children do have a sexuality you know.

Nicola I do . . .

Eve Blue violet, light violet, dark violet, imperial purple.

Nicola . . . and I didn't say they didn't, but . . .

Teddy (*butting in*) How did she lose her hearing by the way?

Greg (*looking at notes*) Fell down the stairs. Query NAI.

Teddy (*heartily*) NAI? CPN? ECT? EDT? ICD? Seems there's no time left for words (*To* **Shirley**.) never mind nouns. Maybe you should do your M Phil on acronyms.

Greg Sorry, Non-Accidental Injury.

Roy Really. What's this got to do with anything.

Nicola (*mildly*) I think that's a good point.

Eve Imperial purple, crimson lake, scarlet lake.

Roy (*pompously*) I'm gratified to see we agree on something Nurse.

Nicola No – about her hearing – (*With her last shred of confidence. Almost apologetically.*) In that, there can be, like we can tend to forget that physical bullying often goes hand in hand with these (*Coughs.*) nurturing so-called relationships.

Eve Deep vermilion, orange chrome.

Teddy I tell you one thing, that cough's an indication of two cancer sticks too many today.

Roy (*brusquely*) Your research is poor, Nurse, without any factual basis. Starting with the ludicrous notion of how many? Are you seriously suggesting that a quarter of the male population should be locked away?

Nicola No, I . . . (*She looks to* **Shirley** *to help her out.*)

Eve Deep cadmium, lemon cadmium.

Shirley I'll just see where the coffee's got to. (*She goes.*)

Greg No, that's not the answer. It's much more complex than that. The family –

Nicola But it's not really 'the family' that's to blame.

Greg (*enthusiastically*) On the contrary, it's part of a very intricate set of family dynamics and family therapy does work. Fathers I've seen, show considerable remorse.

Eve Straw yellow, copper beech, bronze.

Nicola But, I mean, does that surprise you? You know, in front of an authority figure.

Greg (*calmly interrupting*) Okay. Maybe. But I don't feel blame per se is a very healthy approach to rebuilding lives. I agree it happens in all classes but is the product of a dysfunctional family where the man is looking for affection and nurturing, albeit inappropriately, and therefore the whole family, starting with the mother, need re-educating into their appropriate roles.

Teddy (*emphatically*) Tout comprendre est tout pardonner. (*Subtly waving the cigarette smoke away from him.*)

Roy (*agreeing with* **Teddy**) Absolutely.

Nicola If no one takes responsibility.

Greg That's just the point – everyone takes responsibility.

Nicola But then that surely only reinforces the girl's feeling of shame, self disgust and guilt.

Roy Which brings us back to why she felt like that in the first place.

Eve Magenta, brown ochre.

Roy (*sees* **Shirley** *come back into the room*) Ah coffee. Yes? No? Sort of?

Shirley (*brightly*) Coffee will be upon us any second now. And I'm sorry to interrupt but it's just occurred to me that we'd have to take advice about the fire regulations before Dawn could come here. Presumably she can't hear the alarm.

Nicola It's possible to get a flashing light system.

Shirley Fine, but that'll take time to organise.

Roy (*pleased*) Well, that's solved that then.

Greg So that's Rohima and Dave. Okay, thanks very much everyone. Meeting over.

Shirley (*going over to* **Greg**) Can you catch me up on anything I missed that needs minuting? (*She sits next to him.*)

Roy (*putting his notes away in his case*) All that time wasted frittering on.

Eve As soon as they stand up just go.

Evelyn I thought it was a very good discussion. It's so difficult with so many people but very democratic. Only the same conclusion was reached half an hour ago of course. That's the disadvantage of everyone being allowed a say – the time it swallows up.

Roy Oh, Evelyn, I saw your father the other day.

Evelyn (*shocked. Croaks*) He's retired.

Roy I know. But he gave a wonderful paper at a conference.

Evelyn Really?

Roy On bone cancer.

Evelyn Did he?

Roy He's a great man.

Evelyn Umm.

Roy I was very privileged to work under him as a houseman.

Eve Crimson lake, rose pink, flesh pink.

Roy (*inquiringly*) Evelyn? Are you all right?

Evelyn Oh, in the pink, absolutely. Absolutely miles away. (*Suddenly.*) Oh my goodness, is that the time? I'm due at another meeting.

Roy Oh?

Evelyn Working Party on Canine Control.

Roy Oh.

Evelyn Yes, did you know, there are four and a half million litres of dogs' urine floating daily on the surface of Britain?

Lil *enters with a tray of coffee which she puts down.*

Roy Really? You'll have time for a cup of coffee though. (*Turning to* **Nicola**.)

Eve No.

Evelyn Yes, I think so. Just.

Roy (*to* **Nicola**) I don't care what you say we have statistics to prove mothers collude.

Nicola Unfortunately there aren't any which record the women who leave their homes taking their children with them.

Lil *brings two cups of coffee. She stands between* **Roy** *and* **Nicola**. *As* **Nicola** *looks up to take the cup they recognise each other. The cup meant for* **Roy** *accidentally slips from the saucer and into his lap.*

Roy Ah bloody Nora!

Eve *laughs.*

Evelyn Oopps.

Lil I'm sorry, sorry. I'm sorry. Let me get you something to wipe it with. (*She goes.*)

Roy Jesus!

Eve Go. Get out.

Roy *follows* **Lil**, *trying to hold the front of his trousers away from his body.*

Evelyn *makes her way to the door.* **Teddy** *thwarts her escape.*

Teddy Very interesting to be let into this sort of world, a real eye-opener don't you find?

Eve Your brain, Teddy, is the dying throb of a tomcat with tertiary syphilis.

Evelyn (*pleasantly*) Yes. Yes. I suppose it is. I really must be off I'm afraid.

Teddy Thought-provoking question your husband asked the other week.

Evelyn Oh yes?

Teddy It's a great treat to be able to browse through Hansard. I don't often get the chance.

Evelyn Better make the best of it while you can. Before you become a fully fledged leader of the flock.

Teddy Pardon.

Evelyn Flock? Forgive me. How silly. I meant of course when you have your own parish.

Teddy Oh yes. You will come to my induction won't you?

Evelyn I'd love to. Thank you. How exciting.

Eve Will he have to kiss the bishop's ring?

Greg *goes over to* **Evelyn**.

Greg Thanks very much for coming Evelyn.

Evelyn I'm afraid I wasn't able to contribute very much, but anyway I'll see you soon.

Greg Could you just hang on a second. I know Shirley wanted a word with you.

Evelyn What about?

Greg Shirley will explain.

Eve Shirley is a pain in the arse.

Evelyn I'd better go and find her.

Teddy (*watching* **Evelyn** *go, muses*) Good egg, Evelyn. Good egg but absolutely barking mad. (*Then businesslike.*) Now Greg, about this chappie Dave . . .

Greg Teddy, I refuse to be drawn further on the matter. I'm a very old-fashioned fella I'm afraid. I still believe in civil liberties.

Teddy Look, I don't want you to get the impression that I'm a fuss-pot, but being a curate does give one a bit of a high profile. You know what the local press . . .

Shirley (*coming into the room*) Greg, it's Martha from your team. An emergency.

Greg (*calmly*) Excuse me. (*He walks out of the room.*)

Teddy (*to* **Shirley**) I suppose I'd better be making tracks, I've got to drop in on the Mothers' Union.

Shirley Pleased to have you on the team Teddy.

Teddy Good. Splendid. Pleased to be here. I'll give you a ring and arrange a time to go over the demon figures. (*He goes.*)

Shirley Fine. (*To* **Nicola**.) I'm sorry I had to go out for the coffee just then. I thought what you were saying was very thought-provoking.

Nicola (*coldly*) Thank you.

Shirley It's still a very difficult subject. And everyone's so subjective about it.

Nicola I thought you disagreed with objectivity – your dissertation.

Shirley Oh, my thesis – it's more complex than that.

Nicola (*without emotion*) Ah.

Shirley (*looks round*) Oh no, has Evelyn gone?

Nicola She went to look for you.

Shirley I must have a word with her. We can't have the

residents moving into this. (*Gestures at the walls.*) I know she likes decorating. Keep your fingers crossed.

She goes. **Nicola** *is alone.* **Lil** *comes in.* **Nicola** *immediately turns her back, pretending to be intensely interested in the Breughel print.*

Lil Nicola?

Nicola *doesn't turn round.* **Roy** *comes in. The front of his trousers are very wet from where the stain has been sponged. He follows* **Nicola**'*s gaze, positioning himself between her and* **Lil**.

Roy Well I never, my grandmother used to have a reproduction of this in what she used to refer to as her back parlour. I haven't seen it for years.

Lil (*feeling she has to respond*) What a coincidence.

Roy Yes, I'd quite forgotten. My father explained it to me when I was knee-high to a grasshopper. (*Explaining to them, as though they were knee-high to grasshoppers. Pointing.*) You see this person here carries on ploughing the field while the other person, only one leg in view, drowns. (*Then more to himself.*) My father thought it wildly funny but it always made me shiver. Well, fancy remembering a thing . . . (*Then abruptly without warning.*) Are you ready Nurse?

Nicola Yes.

Greg *comes in.*

Greg (*apologetically*) Roy, that was the hospital on the 'phone. Are you available to come with me for a mental health assessment?

Roy (*looking at his trousers*) Now? I can just hear the Appeal Tribunal now 'our client claims that she was sectioned by an incontinent psychiatrist'.

Greg It's between here and the hospital. My car's in the garage. Can I cadge a lift?

Roy By all means. (*He and* **Greg** *walk towards the door. He turns.*) Sorry about this, er, Nurse. You'll be able to find your way back to the hospital on your own won't you?

Nicola Yes Doctor.

Roy *and* **Greg** *go.*

Lil So, you're a nurse.

Nicola (*gathering her things together*) Yes, what did you think I was, a singing telegram?

Lil I didn't know. You could have been anything for all I knew.

Nicola Or cared.

Lil That isn't true. I asked everyone. Even tried to find you – that friend of yours said you'd gone to Spain – to stay with that pen friend. I even . . .

Nicola Spain. Don't be so stupid. You can't go to Spain aged fifteen without a passport. Did you tell the police why I'd left?

Lil We didn't know what to say.

Nicola (*with disgust*) You're still with him?

Lil He's been very sick.

Nicola I could have told you that.

Lil Nicola please, listen.

Nicola Listen? To you? I don't want anything to do with you. Nothing, do you understand? Nothing at all.

Lil But I . . .

Nicola I work from the hospital not here. So it shouldn't be a problem.

Nicola *goes.*

Lil *turns and stares at the blank space where the mirror was and covers her face with her hands.*

Shirley *enters.*

Lil *quickly turns away and starts collecting the cups.*

Shirley (*brightly*) Oh, she's gone. That Nurse. I was going to say she has the same surname as you. Probably just a coincidence.

Lil (*putting the cups on the tray rather frantically*) Probably.

Shirley You're not related are you? Only I thought she looked quite like you.

Lil Was Jane related to Mrs Rochester or was Mrs Rochester part of herself which had to die before she could live happily ever after.

Shirley (*totally confused*) I'm sorry?

Lil Have you ever been in an aeroplane, Shirley?

Shirley (*laughs*) Why yes, of course.

Lil I have, just the once. Well, I tell a lie – I had to come back again. I couldn't get over it. Moving along the runway and the stewardess standing in the aisle demonstrating how to put a life jacket on and this taped voice coming over and nobody except me taking a blind bit of notice. And, then the voice says 'And once in the water, if the life jacket fails to inflate, blow into this tube!' And I'm thinking (*With panic.*) In the water! Once I'm in the water! And I'm imagining myself struggling in the ocean with the duff life jacket but nobody else is even listening. They are too busy rooting out their credit cards for their duty frees.

Evelyn and **Eve** *re-enter.*

Shirley (*confused*) Oh, yes, of course, you said. Your daughter's an air hostess.

Lil (*picking up the tray*) Don't mind me, I read too much. (*She goes.*)

Evelyn She's gone up in the world then?

Shirley Lil?

Evelyn No, this mythical daughter. She told me once she was a hairdresser. What do you make of that?

Shirley I don't think it's any of our business.

Evelyn She's a liar.

Shirley Now what do you make of this? (*Meaning the room.*)

Eve What are you doing in this place?

Evelyn It's better to use gloss over this sort of paint than emulsion otherwise it will just show through. I don't mind doing it.

Eve Why do you have to open your big mouth.

Shirley (*pleased*) Would you? It would save a lot of time and money.

Evelyn Actually I'm always pleased to do practical things rather . . . I'm not very good with people.

Shirley Oh, I wouldn't say that.

Scene Three

In sickness and in health

Lil's *kitchen diner. That evening.*

Tony, *her husband, sits in front of the TV.* **Lil** *puts* **Tony**'s *meal of steamed fish, broccoli and brown bread on a plate. She places it on a tray with a knife and fork and puts it on his lap.*

Tony (*appreciatively*) Thanks. (*He closes his eyes and takes a mouthful of fish.*)

Lil What are you doing?

Tony Pretending it's cod in batter.

Lil (*smiles*) Unfortunately it weren't on the diet sheet the doctor gave me. Did the District Nurse call today?

Tony I'll say. It wasn't the usual one, a slip of a girl. Highlight of my day.

Lil (*gently disapproving*) Tony.

Tony (*mildly*) Apart from you she's the only person I've seen all week. What's the matter? Jealous?

Lil (*sits down in an armchair*) No. It's just. I don't like you talking like that.

Tony Give over. It's the sort of thing any bloke would say.

Lil I suppose.

She picks up her book and starts to read. **Tony** *continues to eat and watch the telly. But she can't concentrate.*

Tony?

Tony Um. What?

Lil Nothing. (*Pause.*) You know when you went into hospital I was very frightened that I, that I might lose you.

Tony I know. (*Slight pause.*) But there's life in the old dog yet, don't you worry.

Lil I wanted. (*Deep breath.*) When Nicola left home.

Tony (*groans*) Oh Lil.

Lil Please. Don't get upset. What she said.

Tony (*tense*) Yes.

Lil (*almost apologetically*) Was there, (*Slight pause.*) I'm only asking, any truth in it?

Tony (*flatly*) No. Why bring that up now?

Lil I want to know. Now.

Tony You asked me then and I told you.

Lil Why d'you suppose she said things like that then?

Tony Why are you asking me all of a sudden? You seemed sure at the time.

Lil I didn't believe it. (*Pause.*) It's not the sort of thing you tackle someone you love about when you want to believe them, anyway. But, (*Hesitates.*)

Tony (*reasonably*) She did it out of spite – pure malice. She never liked me. Right from the beginning – remember the fuss when you changed her surname to mine.

Lil It seemed the best thing years ago. I didn't want her to face awkward questions at school. We hadn't had it easy.

Tony She resented me. She resented our relationship. She wanted to split us up – it's never been the same since – has it? Oh I know, it's all right but I catch you looking at me from time to time and I think, if it hadn't been for her vindictiveness. Still, what's done is done. (*Pause.*) There. You can get on with your novel now.

Lil (*pause*) It does go on, not that we ever used to hear about it. It's in all the papers.

Tony (*slowly*) And leaving some innocent couples with their lives in ruins.

Lil (*this is difficult*) What d'you s'pose the men who did do it say when their wives ask them?

Tony How the hell should I know? (*Slight pause.*) Unless of course you think that I do. Is that it?

Lil Sometimes people have affairs for years without their wives or husbands knowing.

Tony What are you saying; you've had an affair?

Lil No, no. That's not it.

Tony (*sighs*) If it was true, why didn't she tell you?

Lil She did.

Tony Only as a garbled excuse when you caught her flying out of the door with her bag packed. Why not before?

Lil Maybe she was frightened.

Tony Frightened? Lil, have I ever raised my hand to you?

Lil No. That's why you were different. Why I couldn't believe my luck. But why?

Tony (*sighs*) You took her to the Doctor once didn't you?

Lil (*surprised*) Yes, yes I did.

Tony What did he say?

Lil She said she was allergic to soap.

Tony And you believed the doctor?

Lil Yes.

Tony But you don't live with the doctor. Look Lil you know everything about me. We don't have any secrets. I tried hard remember? She just didn't like me. Every Friday I'd buy her something on my way home from work.

Lil I know.

Tony I wasn't able to win her trust or affection.

Lil (*sighs*) No.

Tony Can we leave it? Arguing and open heart surgery don't go together as well as steamed fish and broccoli.

Lil Sorry.

Pause. She picks up her book.

Tony I can't imagine why you brought all this up.

Lil (*pause*) I saw her today.

Tony Who?

Lil (*pause*) Nicola.

Long pause.

Tony Where?

Lil At work. She's a nurse.

Tony What did she say?

Lil She wouldn't speak to me.

Tony Oh.

Scene Four

St Dymphna's

Ten days later.

The mirror has not yet been replaced but the walls have been repainted and the room looks 'homely'.

Lil *is cleaning the windows. The curtains lie on the back of the chair.*

Shirley *enters.*

Shirley (*surprised to see* **Lil** *alone*) Oh, I thought Dave was in here.

Lil I think he's gone to make a cup of tea.

Shirley (*lowering her voice a little*) How is he?

Lil He seems to be settling in OK.

Shirley Has he said anything?

Lil Not much. Yes and no. Please and thank you.

Shirley He's not said a word to me since he arrived. See if you can . . .

She stops as **Dave** *enters carrying two cups of tea and quickly changes the subject.*

The new mirror should arrive sometime today. Do you know where Rohima is? I'm supposed to be giving her a lift to the DSS.

Dave (*puts the two cups down on the coffee table next to the armchair and sits down*) She was here a few minutes ago I've just made her a cup of tea.

Shirley *and* **Lil** *exchange a glance.*

Lil She went out to post a letter.

Dave *takes a mouthful of tea and appears to have some difficulty swallowing it.*

Shirley Are you OK, Dave?

Dave (*smiles ruefully*) One of the disadvantages of being a state registered junkie is the side effects. Although one of the advantages admittedly is that I've never had to steal to support the habit. Don't look so surprised I can speak but it's just that until today I didn't want to.

Shirley Would you like me to suggest to Dr Freeman that he reduce your medication?

Dave I reckon it's the reduction in the tablets that's made me like this. Cold Turkey or is that a frightfully outmoded phrase? I'm a bit out of date with street jargon.

He laughs which causes some pain in his chest. He tries not to draw attention to this but **Shirley** *notices.*

Shirley (*concerned*) Are you sure you're all right?

Dave If there's one thing experience has taught me, it's that once you have the label 'nutter' and you complain of physical ailments, they certify you before they operate.

Shirley Is something wrong then?

Dave Oh, take no notice, I'm being facetious. The tea was too hot, that's all. I'm fine. Honestly.

Shirley (*unsure*) If you say so.

Dave (*firmly*) I do. Thank you.

Shirley OK. Well, I'd better see where Rohima is. (*To* **Lil**.) And then I've got to take some things to Greg's office. The number's on the list by the 'phone if you need me. (*To them both.*) See you later.

She goes. **Lil** *contiues to work. Silence.*

Lil That's the most I've ever heard you say Dave. Why haven't you spoken before?

Dave Under the scrutiny of the psychiatric profession each syllable is weighed, waiting to be labelled before it's even uttered. Such meaning is heaped upon the spoken word that one becomes too inhibited to perform the act. Humour – that's a no-go area. And as for flippancy, try that out on them and they look at you as if you're about to self-destruct. Genuine emotion is so painful that it's reduced to self-conscious clichés.

Lil Well don't mind me, I'm not one of them. Wax as lyrical as you like.

Dave I'm sure half my life has been wonderful. I just can't remember it. All I can recall when I'm well is the minutiae of long stay institutionalised existence. The intensity of feelings over such tiny discoveries like the far-reaching ecstasy of turning over the pillow to find the cooler side. The heartfelt relief of not getting the first or the last cup of tea out of that humungous pot. The throat closing joy of knowing that the biscuits have three layers this week. All these petty but all the same deeply felt things take on a passionate poetry of their own. (*Slight pause.*) Very boring really.

Lil Carry on, it's nice to see you so chatty.

Dave But that's about all I know – institutions. Have you ever been in one?

Lil Butlins? (*They both laugh.*)

Dave I don't suppose you'd care to sit down and have this cup of tea which is going to waste?

Lil All right if you don't mind me mending these. (*She takes the curtains and a sewing box. She sits down in the other chair and starts to repair the hem of the curtains.*) Now you've gone all quiet on me. Your life must have had a little more variety.

Dave Let me see. Oh yes, in 1961 I was put in prison for being an unneighbourly bugger.

Lil (*surprised*) Were you under 21 then?

Dave I'll take that as a compliment thank you. But no, the law wasn't changed till '67. We were both the same age, 30. He, Jon, had a so-called prestigious job in local government and had been paying a proportion of his salary to a person who threatened to go to the press. (*Matter-of-factly.*) It happened quite a lot in those days. By the time Jon got round to telling me, we were living together by then, and I said, well I can't remember exactly what I said but the gist of it was to call this person's bluff and stop paying. (*Laughingly.*) I must have been mad. I don't know how I managed to delude myself that spite doesn't exist for spite's sake when it so obviously does.

Lil Do you really think so?

Dave Yes, don't you?

Lil I don't know.

Dave Take my word for it or do you think the world revolves on revenge?

Lil But hadn't you done something to this person?

Dave I don't even know who they were to this day. There was a scandal of course. Jon lost his job. We both did. We were sent to jail. You don't want to hear about this. Tell me about Butlins.

Lil Yes I do. What was your job?

Dave I worked in the soft furnishings department of a shop in the West End. My father nearly had an apoplectic fit. First throwing all his hopes of an army career away and then the downright disgrace and perversion of living with Jon. God, at least it took the abuse partially away from my mother. But Christ, have I paid for not opting into his world.

Lil What happened when you got out of prison?

Dave We were out of work. Jon felt the shame more than I did. He couldn't get a job, none of the people he'd worked with would speak to him. A year after our release he killed himself.

Lil Oh, I'm sorry.

Dave (*pragmatically*) Perhaps clichés are clichés because they happen too often.

Lil Is that, I mean after his death, is that when you became ill?

Dave I'd had a nervous breakdown before I met him. If you were privy to my medical records you'd see an entry which reads 'time of stability whilst living with friend'. After his death I had another breakdown, yes. And since, everything out there has got better but I've missed it. I've come out to be greeted by exactly the same climate as I left. And why should I feel so indignant? I haven't contributed anything to making it better. I haven't fought for anything, I've done nothing.

Lil You're not in the minority then are you? (*No response.*) Dave?

Dave If I was in the position to analyse myself I might conclude that I was struggling between dignity and despair. (*Pause. Then very cheerfully.*) But tomorrow is another day isn't that what they say and it's never too late and all those things. (*Slight pause.*) Lil, you look so sad.

Lil You don't tell happy stories.

Dave So now, holiday camps – is the excitement intense?

Lil No, it's in chalets.

Dave Go on then.

Lil Aw, there's nothing to say. Just, we had a lovely time.

Dave Who's we?

Lil Tony took me and my daughter there a few months after I'd met him. She was only six. I'd been married before. She was just old enough to go into shops on her own. And she bought me a birthday present that she'd chosen herself for the first time. Only she was so excited she couldn't wait till my birthday to give it to me. Silly the things you remember.

Dave What was it?

Lil A magnet.

Dave (*laughs*) I wonder what Dr Freeman would make of that.

Lil Actually it was a magnet tied to a piece of string wrapped up in a shoebox with ten paper fish that she'd drawn and cut out herself and put a paperclip on the end of their noses and she showed me how to play fishing. I don't know where she got the idea – school I suppose. For ages afterwards every Sunday after we'd had supper and washed up we used to sit together on the kitchen table, put the fish on the floor and take it in turns to reel them in.

Dave I don't remember my parents spending any time with us at all but then my memory isn't cracked up too much.

Lil You have brothers and sisters then?

Dave Two brothers. At least I started out with two brothers. I haven't seen them for years. Last I heard one of them was working for a bank in America and the other one was a naval officer.

Lil My first husband was in the Navy. He wasn't an officer or anything. Just an ordinary seaman.

Dave Rum lot was he?

Lil Oh yeah and he liked a drink an' all. When he came home on leave it was like, after the first day, he couldn't stand the sight of me. They got used to my face in the Casualty Department. I don't think there was a law against it then. Certainly there was nowhere to go. When he got out of the Navy altogether it was awful, my home was like a prison. At one time I thought we'd never get away.

Dave But you did. To Butlins with Tony.

Lil Yes. He taught me to dance while we were there. I was so het-up about making a mistake. He'd just laugh. He was like that about everything. Easy going. 'What's the point of being so worried about getting it right that you can't enjoy yourself', he'd say to me. He never lost his temper over anything, big or small. (*Then.*) Oh dear, I don't know how you got me onto all this.

Dave Are you still married to him?

Lil Oh yes.

Dave Only you said 'was'.

Lil Oh he is. He's still like that. (*Slight pause.*) Dave? You know what you were saying about (**Teddy** *enters right.*) spite –

Teddy Is Shirley about? Sorry I didn't . . .

Lil I think she's gone to look for Rohima.

Dave (*winks at* **Lil**) Of course the hardware department was the most sought-after to work in but I preferred soft furnishings. Its allure is so theatrical. (*Picks up a curtain. Mimes ripping the curtain in a theatrical fashion.*) Three and a quarter yards for you modom? (*This exertion causes him some pain which he tries to conceal.*)

Teddy I'll just go and check. I think I've left my lights on anyway.

Dave (*to* **Lil**) Sorry about that. The devil got into me.

Lil (*laughs*) His lights may be on but there's no one at home. Sorry I didn't mean . . .

Dave (*laughs*) It's all right. What were you going to say? Before?

Lil Oh yes. Will casserole be all right for supper? (*She stands, starts folding the curtains.*)

Dave I thought we were supposed to get our own meals?

Lil One meal a week I prepare. And I'm running late.

Dave That wasn't what you wanted to ask.

Lil Some other time. I must get on.

Leaves curtains on chair and scissors.

Dave Okay.

Lil See you the day after tomorrow. (*She looks at him.*) Dave, do you feel all right?

Dave Just tired. Time for my afternoon kip I think.

Lil *goes off left,* **Teddy** *meets* **Shirley** *in the hallway right.*

Teddy (*urgently*) Oh Shirley, there you are. I've been wanting to have a quiet word with you all day.

Shirley Can't it wait Teddy? I'm just about . . .

Teddy This is urgent I'm afraid. I'll have to resign from the Management Committee.

Shirley Teddy, you can't do that. Well, I mean, I suppose you can but you've only just joined us. Why the change of heart?

Teddy News has reached my ears, actually someone told me, that a man called here wearing a frock. Don't you see? If this place attracts that sort of attention. It's my reputation. Well, it's not mine – the Church's. You know what the papers are like and it's not just the tabloids these days. Even the noun bachelor is all innuendo.

Shirley (*slight pause as she looks at* **Teddy** *who's wearing a cassock*) Words fail me. (*Then.*) Who told you a man wearing a dress came to the door?

Teddy The Churchwarden's wife heard it from the WI and they heard it from a member of the PCC. Sorry, Parochial Church Council. I can't name names you understand.

Shirley Please think it over. At least see this week out. I've been doing the accounts for last month and I'm only half-way through.

Teddy (*guiltily*) Oh, I know I shouldn't just up and leave you in the lurch.

Shirley I suppose I could ask Greg.

Teddy (*blasé*) What does he know, all he cares about is people. (*Decides.*) All right, point taken. I'll have a stab at totting up the figures. But we must find a time to discuss this more fully.

Shirley Thanks. They're in my office. The cleaning receipts are in the cupboard in the living room.

He goes. **Evelyn/Eve** *enter right.*

Ah, Evelyn. Just the person.

Eve Careful.

Evelyn Hello Shirley . . .

Shirley I've got to go out. I shouldn't be too long but we are destined to have a call from a couple on behalf of the local Ratepayers' Association. Would you see them and give them the benefit of your diplomacy?

Evelyn Me?

Shirley If you don't mind.

Eve I do mind.

Evelyn What about Teddy?

Shirley I, er, think you're eminently a better choice. Just listen to what they have to say and explain how necessary this place is.

Evelyn How?

Shirley (*curtly*) Try, if at all possible, to put the liberal point of view.

Eve She hates you.

Evelyn I resent that. My husband toyed quite sleeplessly with the SDP for a while.

Eve Liar.

Shirley Sorry. This is your afternoon here isn't it? It won't take long. All you have to do is make them a cup of tea. You can show them the living room and the kitchen but don't show them the residents' bedrooms. I'm sorry but I'm in a bit of a rush. Rohima's waiting for me in the car.

Evelyn But what about. . . ?

Shirley Don't worry Steve's at work, Eric is on a course and won't be back until late this evening and Dave usually takes himself off for a sleep in his room in the afternoon. Thanks very much.

Evelyn Shirley, I'd love to but I'm afraid/

Shirley (*not hearing*) And thanks very much for doing the decorating. You'll find your painting things in a carrier bag in the kitchen. See you later.

Shirley *goes out right.* **Evelyn** *goes to the kitchen left.* **Teddy**

enters the living room. **Dave** *looks asleep in the chair. He opens his eyes as* **Teddy** *tiptoes in.*

Teddy All right? Didn't mean to disturb you. Sorry. Just got to get something from the cupboard.

Dave (*yawns*) Would . . . could you give me a hand to my room?

Teddy (*bluffingly cheerful*) You're all right having a snooze there. Not to worry – it's your home after all.

Dave (*sighs*) Lil.

Teddy Pardon?

Dave Would you please tell Lil, I'm sorry about the seaman.

Teddy (*with fear*) What? (*He quickly leaves the room.*)

Dave And say thanks.

Teddy *has already gone. He paces the hallway.*

Teddy (*calls*) Lil? Lil? Where are you?

Lil (*runs towards him onion and knife in hand. Worried*) What is it?

Teddy I don't know how to say it – it isn't a very pleasant task.

Lil Don't hold back. The gamut of my curriculum vitae runs from nappies to incontinence pads – only a few of us are left dealing with our own shit in the meantime. What is it? A dog turd through the letter box?

Teddy No, but something equally unpleasant.

Lil What? Where?

Teddy On the upholstery I think. Culpable emission – an accident I'm sure.

Lil (*impatiently*) You what?

Teddy (*very embarrassed*) Bodily fluid. Male.

Lil (*with disbelief*) Are you trying to tell me someone's wanked over my loose covers?

Teddy Brutally speaking, yes.

Lil Are you playing with a full deck?

Teddy (*lowering his voice*) Please try and be discreet about it.

Lil I can't do anything right this minute I've only got one pair of hands unless of course you'd . . .

Teddy No, no, I've got plenty to be getting on with. (*He goes left.*)

Lil So've I.

Lil *raises her eyes to the ceiling. Sighs. She follows* **Teddy** *and meets* **Evelyn/Eve** *coming towards her.* **Evelyn** *is holding a carrier bag.*

Evelyn (*very friendly*) What's got into Teddy?

Lil Don't ask me. St Dymphna's. Huh. Tower of Babel more like.

Evelyn I'm sorry?

Lil You know, that story in the Bible where no one understands what anyone else is saying and the whole thing collapses.

Evelyn Lil, I'd like you to do me a big favour?

Lil (*not unkindly*) Depends what it is.

Evelyn Shirley wants me to see two people who are going to call this afternoon who want to know something about this place. Would you see them for me?

Lil If Shirley asked you that's who she wanted to meet them. If she'd wanted me to talk to them she'd have asked me.

Evelyn I wouldn't ask but –

Lil I'm sorry Evelyn but I probably couldn't answer their questions. You're on the Management Committee, you're the ideal person.

Evelyn It's just that I might not be able to wait all afternoon.

Lil You should have explained that to Shirley. I won't be here myself, I'm due at the Sparidae project in less than an hour. If you don't mind me saying I do think it's important that you hang on here. It's obviously a public relations exercise. I'll show you where the tea things are kept if you like.

Evelyn Please Lil/

Lil It's not my place it's yours.

Lil *goes leaving* **Evelyn** *alone.*

Evelyn *stands, looking out.* **Eve** *stands beside her looking out.*

Interval

Scene Five

St Dymphna's

Richard *and* **Gaynor Brittain**, *the rate-payers, stand nervously in the hallway preparing their thoughts.*

Richard (*practising his speech*) I do understand and I'm very sympathetic. However, my wife and I, no, no, Gaynor and I, have been elected to speak for, no, no – on behalf of – a group of us who are concerned about the social problems in the area. I mean the safety of the residents is uppermost in our minds, no, no, not the community at large. I mean those in here. They're at risk from threats, general intimidation, riots – we had a riot only a couple of miles away in '81.

(*Lapsing into his own thoughts.*) It's not as if I'm one of those people who continually checks how much their house is worth. It would be too depressing, now the market's slumped and what with the threat of the Channel Tunnel Rail Link, the extension of the South Circular and Docklands Light Railway. A place like this, plonked in the same road is hardly likely to improve the situation, remove

the blight. It doesn't bear thinking about. I've worked all
my life to maintain my mortgage. It's not as if I'm able to
earn thousands and thousands of pounds. I missed out on
that band wagon. Not that I want to make a career lusting
after money. I could do with a break as a matter of fact
but whatever else my working life has been, it's been one
long scramble to earn enough. Even now the kids are gone
– and Gaynor wasn't able to cope as I thought she would.
She told me she worked in a nursery. I'd got round to
proposing before I discovered it was a flower sort but
somehow my original idea that she must be good with
children stuck. She now works three days a week in a
Garden Centre in Lofton Park. Huh, and she had to settle
long ago for the fact that I wasn't a climber. No, I wasn't
going to reach the top and be able to sit on my laurels
contemplating the view. I've just managed to reach a little
ledge which now threatens to crumble beneath the weight
of everyone else who's trying to cling on, pulling me down
with them in the process. My wife's never been what you
might call solid as a rock in the upstairs department. She's
always been rather edgy. Living close to people who are
really disturbed might tip the balance. She might go mad.
My daughter might take drugs. My son might get AIDS
and I've worked all my life to be a normal family man.
(*Pulling himself together.*) Good afternoon, my name is
Richard Brittain. It's not that I don't understand it's just
that I can't see any alternative. Can you give me
permission to feel less afraid?

Gaynor (*practising her speech*) I do understand and believe
me we're very sympathetic but we have been asked. It's
not that I've got anything against people who've had
nervous breakdowns. (*Lapsing into her own thoughts.*) In fact
I nearly had one myself once only the doctor got to me just
in time and the Valium got to me sooner. I'd not thought
about it until we did the fortnight's shopping. We do it
together these days which is nice. Besides, they all seem to
be built a car ride away. Sort of ranch like places in the
middle of open concrete.

It was a young woman with two toddlers, reminded me of
myself. I thought, I should write a book I should. I stood

racking my brains for a title when it struck me 'Let's Go
Mad In Safeways'. I rather liked it. We were behind her
you see, biscuits to the left of us, crisps and Hula Hoops to
the right, when I sent Richard back. We'd picked up the
unmicrowavable lasagne by mistake. Well, he had.

The elder one of these toddlers had just recovered from a
tantrum at not being able to gain the enviable position of
the shopping trolley seat which was now triumphantly
occupied by the younger one. I couldn't swear to the
gender, it's so difficult with these Benetton and what-not
designer clothes, but the tantrum one was called Jack
because the woman kept droning, 'Put those back, Jack' as
he was busy collecting as many packets of crisps as his
chubby fingers could grasp and she was automatically
snatching them back, replacing them haphazardly on the
top shelves amongst the gravy granules and the custard
powder.

When it dawned on Jack that this was no longer a game,
he threw himself flat on the floor in front of the trolley and
screamed – in that way that goes right through you – she
said so blankly, 'Come on Jack, get up' and a variety of
matter-of-fact coaxing until with her teeth firmly gritted
together she says, 'Don't say I didn't warn you' and
pushes the trolley forward regardless. He just managed to
roll out of the way unhurt but screamed even louder. It
made my stomach lurch. I thought, Jesus God, let's hope
there's not a Social Worker in the shop and my heart went
out to her because I knew how she felt.

My children have grown up now. My eldest daughter's got
a girl of her own. I didn't want to work when they were
small, I wanted to make the most of them, you never get
that time again do you? You don't bargain for the sleepless
nights, snatching half a tin of apple puree for lunch and
never going out in the evening, until it was me who
insisted. My brother was at college in London and he'd
come over to babysit.

It only came out at Christmas when my daughter refused
to take the baby over to his house. Why didn't you tell me
then? She said, 'Because he threatened me with ridiculous

things but when you're small you believe them'. 'But', I said, 'Didn't you say no?' She virtually spat back, and she's not like that with me normally, 'Saying no to a grown man makes no difference unless you're trying to make me feel I said no in the wrong way'. 'Of course not', I said.

Oh I should have seen the signs. She used to wake up with bad dreams. Cling to me on the one evening a week we'd go out, but I thought it was because I'd never been out without her since she was born.

I said, 'But he's got kids of his own now.' She said, 'Yes. I don't want anything to do with him.' I said, 'But you used to go over there at Christmas.' She said, 'Yes but that was before the baby was born.' Then she said, 'Don't say anything. You won't tell Dad will you?' I said, 'I don't know what to do.' She said, 'I don't want any fuss, I don't want them looking at me thinking – whatever they will be thinking. I don't want anyone to know.'

And I haven't said anything. I blame myself. I shouldn't have been so selfish wanting to go out but I was desperate. I must have been a little crazy in those days. He was my own brother. After she told me I can't stop thinking about it. I don't want to. It drives me mad.

Evelyn *comes along the passageway to greet them.* **Richard** *gives* **Gaynor**'s *hand a reassuring squeeze.* **Eve** *sizes up* **Evelyn**'s *performance.*

Evelyn Hello, I'm sorry to have kept . . .

Richard Good afternoon my name is Richard.

Gaynor (*nervously*) And, I'm his wife, Gaynor.

Evelyn I'm Evelyn. I'm sorry but I'm afraid Shirley has been unavoidably called away but I'm on the Management Committee and I hope I'll do.

Richard Pleased to meet you.

Gaynor Pleased to meet you.

Evelyn I'm sure you'll understand but I can't show you all the way round (*She goes into the room.*) because people live here, it is their home – but I can show you the sitting room. Please come through.

They go into the living room. **Evelyn** *turns unconsciously obscuring their view of* **Dave** *who looks asleep in the chair, his cup of tea lies on its side, its contents split.* **Evelyn** *acts normally.* **Eve** *jumps back in fear.*

Gaynor (*to* **Richard** *pointing at the picture*) Oh look darling. Do you remember when we first moved, we borrowed that picture from the library. (*To* **Evelyn**.) Those were the days before you could buy reasonable prints.

Eve (*turns to look at* **Dave**) He's dead. He's dead!

Evelyn I'm afraid the mirror got broken and we're still waiting for a replacement.

Eve Stop being so polite, that man in that chair there has died.

Gaynor (*thoughtless*) Not a very welcoming omen.

Richard (*tightly*) Dear? (*Then pleasantly to* **Evelyn**.) It's not that we're . . .

Gaynor (*ruefully*) Not for the first seven years at least.

Evelyn Can I get you a cup of coffee? (*Gesturing them towards the door left.*)

Eve Try and say excuse me but I think something's wrong and I can't cope.

Evelyn (*unnerved*) Please come through to the kitchen. The kettle's boiled and you can see what it looks like. (*Turns to go into the kitchen.*)

Eve Don't just pretend it's all right.

Gaynor (*follows*) Don't get me wrong, we always donate to charity. Despite any financial crisis that might occur I've never turned anyone away on the doorstep with an empty envelope or switched the telly off without ringing in our credit card number for that matter.

Richard No it's not for ourselves. (*Sees* **Dave**.) I say is that chap all right?

Evelyn (*takes two paces back but doesn't look at* **Dave**) Oh Dave. I didn't see him there. He often drops off in the afternoon.

Eve starts to refer to herself in the third person.

Eve Are you mad? Are you mad? You are mad!

Eve weeps.

Richard (*takes* **Dave**'s *hand and tries to find his pulse. Simply*) He's dead.

Gaynor *instinctively turns away. Puts her hand in front of her mouth.*

Evelyn (*looks at* **Dave**) What? (*Shakes him.*) Oh God, wake up Dave! What shall I do? (*She goes.*)

Gaynor I'd 'phone for an ambulance if I were you.

Evelyn Yes . . . yes . . . (*Exits.*)

Richard (*after her*) That's no good. They'll refuse to budge him. He's cold.

Gaynor Come on Richard, come away. Don't touch him.

Richard (*ashen*) Somehow I don't think it's appropriate to continue our visit.

They go to the door right and meet **Teddy** *coming in.*

Gaynor You're too late Father. He's passed over.

Teddy I beg your pardon.

Richard Gaynor. That's probably what he's here for. (*To* **Teddy**.) All in a day's work for you I expect. (*He puts his arm round* **Gaynor**'s *shoulders and they go.*) Rather you than me.

Teddy *stares at* **Dave**. *Immobilised by fear.* **Evelyn/Eve** *come back into the room.*

Teddy (*numb*) How?

Evelyn (*shakily*) I don't know. But he is. We can't leave him here.

Teddy You should ring a doctor.

Evelyn I have rung the hospital. Roy. He's dealing with it. The ambulance. He's with my father.

Teddy Best not to touch him then.

Evelyn But he's dead.

Teddy How do you know?

Evelyn (*voice rising*) He's not breathing is he?

Teddy (*blankly*) He should never have been let out of hospital.

Evelyn The others mustn't find him here. Please you must help me. We should put him in his own room.

Teddy I can't.

Evelyn Why not?

Teddy I can't touch him.

Evelyn Please.

Teddy He disgusts me. 'Men leaving the natural use of the woman, burn with lust for one another and are paid in their own persons the fitting wage for such provisions.' I can't do anything for him.

Evelyn Teddy.

Teddy Romans. We all have a choice Evelyn either to stick by what we believe in or distort it to suit our own ends.

Evelyn God. (*Calling to* **Eve**.) Please help me.

Teddy It's my faith Evelyn. I can't be shaken from it.

Lil (*VO*) Would somebody come to the door it's the mirror.

Teddy The Press!! (*Then to* **Evelyn**.) Don't let them know I'm here. They'll have a field day if they find me here.

He goes as **Lil** *comes in carrying the mirror.*

Lil I don't give much for his episcopal potential. (*Then seeing* **Dave**.) What happened?

Eve Don't let her blame you.

Lil (*goes over to* **Dave**) Dave? (*Tries to find his pulse.*)
He's . . .

Evelyn I know.

She turns and walks away.

Scene Six

Three in one

Roy's *office*. **George** *flicks through some case notes*. **Roy** *enters,
carrying two cups of tea. He gives one to* **George**.

George You were the last person I was expecting to bump
into.

Roy The mother's on my admission ward. At first I
thought it was a ploy to get into the same hospital. But our
records show she was admitted once before, some years
ago, obsessive personality. Seems she had psychotherapy
in between. Now she thinks the child got cancer following
her divorce – stress.

George Well she saw something, a review of my book or
something in the paper and asked the child's consultant to
get in touch with me. Very well educated I thought; and
asked all the right questions. I'm only sorry to have had to
confirm the original diagnosis. Such a pretty child.

Roy I was hoping, well, I was hoping if the child had a
better prognosis so would Mrs Derwent. When she's not
blaming herself she's compulsively reeling off lists of what
they've eaten to me, all organically grown wholefoods.

George (*dryly*) If the reports one reads every other day in
the papers are anything to go by the only healthy way to
die is to starve oneself. How's life treating you?

Roy Much the same. I'm very flattered that you
remembered me after all this time.

George Never forgotten you dear boy. You're wasted in psychiatry, you know that don't you? Made the choice too young.

Roy It's very kind of you to say so but . . . (*The phone rings.*) Excuse me. (**Roy** *picks it up irritably.*) Freeman. Joan, I thought I said no calls. (*Pause.*) Oh, I see. Yes of course. Put her through. (*To* **George**.) It's Evelyn, your daughter. (*Offering the receiver.*)

George It can't be for me. She doesn't know I'm here.

Roy (*on the phone*) Evelyn. What a coincidence. Guess who's with me? Your father. Would you – (*Pause.*) Oh I see. (*Pause.*) Are you sure? (*Pause.*) Yes, of course. Don't worry. I'll deal with it straight away. I'm sorry. It must have been a terrible shock. (*Pause.*) Thank you. 'Bye.

George Something happened?

Roy The group home where she does some voluntary work. One of the patients has died. She found the body.

George Oh dear. How did she sound?

Roy Very calm and competent. Excuse me. (*He presses the intercom on his telephone.*) Joan? Can you get on to ambulance control? One of my patients has died at Headsend Road. We're going to have to get him out quickly. Explain the set-up there and see if you can persuade the crew to take him – I don't want any nonsense. In the circumstances waiting around for undertakers is out of the question. Any problems please get straight back to me. (*To* **George**.) I am sorry about this.

George Not at all. I do remember what it's like.

Greg *knocks before entering.*

Greg The file you wanted on Ruth Derwent.

Roy You took your time. We've finished discussing her now.

Greg I'm sorry. I was in a meeting. I didn't get the message until . . .

Roy (*joking*) Well I hope you're not going back into one. (*To* **George**.) Social workers. The bane of our lives.

George And consciences.

Roy (*seriously*) I've just had a phone call Greg. Bad news. St Dymphna's. (*Gently.*) It seems Dave died this afternoon.

Greg (*genuinely*) Oh, I am sorry . . . How? . . .

Roy I think we should go over there. Unfortunately my wife's got the car today.

Greg Mine's still in the garage.

Roy Go and ask that Nurse Cretsley – she's on the ward. She's got a car. It'll be good experience for her to come with us.

Greg All right. I've got supervision with Martha now. I'll just have to let her know. (*He goes.*)

George I'll leave you to it.

Roy Unless you'd like to come over to St Dymphna's and meet Evelyn?

George (*lightly*) I think Evelyn sees quite enough of me as it is. Besides I said I'd drop in on Morpeth-Jones while I was here.

Roy Maybe I should get him to talk to Mrs Derwent. According to him we're all predetermined from the womb. He blames DNA for everything.

George (*stands. Quizzically*) St Dymphna's?

Roy The name of the hostel. Not my choosing. Patron saint of the insane apparently.

George What on earth did she do to deserve that?

Roy I didn't know either. It took the local curate to enlighten me. She's supposed to have left home after her mother died and her father turned his attentions to her, so the story goes. He caught up with her and proposed marriage. When she refused he cut her head off. And she became enshrined or whatever they call it in the thirteenth century.

George (*laughs*) God help us all.

Roy Quite.

Scene Seven

St Dymphna's

Shirley, **Lil** and **Evelyn/Eve**. **Lil** *picks up* **Dave**'s *tea-cup and wipes up the spilt tea.*

Shirley I should have taken more notice.

Lil Don't blame yourself. You weren't to know.

Shirley I had no idea.

Lil I can't believe it.

Shirley I should have done something.

Lil But he was so well, in himself, I mean. Talkative.

Shirley Tried to persuade him to see someone.

Lil (*cuts the string around the mirror*) I didn't know anything was wrong. I didn't expect.

Shirley You don't have to do that Lil.

Lil I've got to do something. I can't bear to think about it.

Shirley Evelyn, are you OK?

Roy, **Greg** and **Nicola** arrive. **Lil** *puts the scissors down on a chair.*

Roy We came over as soon as was humanly possible. Nurse, do you think you could organize a cup of tea for us all?

Lil I'll do it.

Roy Please be careful how you bring it in. (*To* **Shirley**.) Did the ambulance agree to take him?

Shirley Yes.

Roy Good. I had a word with them.

Eve Words.

Shirley There's something sadly final about a silent ambulance. The police took a short statement.

Greg And?

Shirley There wasn't much to say. (*To* **Roy**.) Why, I mean, how did he die?

Roy We won't know that until after the post mortem. I was rather hoping you'd be able to tell me.

Evelyn *sits down, first taking the scissors off the chair. She holds them in her hand.*

Shirley Me?

Roy You were here weren't you?

Shirley No I . . .

Greg Who was here?

Evelyn No one. No one.

Shirley Evelyn.

Roy What happened Evelyn?

Eve Careful.

Evelyn Nothing.

Greg (*to* **Shirley**) Where were you?

Roy (*to* **Evelyn**) Nothing?

Shirley (*to* **Greg**) I took Rohima to the DSS.

Eve In the counting house counting out the money.

Roy You're supposed to be a house manager not a taxi driver.

Shirley She agreed to claim benefit. I thought I'd give her a lift.

Roy And it had to be today?

Shirley It seemed too good an opportunity to miss.

Greg Where is she now?

Shirley She's still there. She's coming back on the bus. Oh God, what'll I tell her?

Evelyn Do you have to say anything?

Roy You saw him before you went out?

Shirley Yes of course. (*To* **Evelyn**.) Of course I do.

Roy And you couldn't see anything wrong? Fit as a fiddle one minute, drops dead the next.

Nicola (*to* **Roy**) He did complain of breathing problems and chest pains while he was on the ward.

Roy He felt claustrophobic, that's why I wanted him moved.

Greg (*to* **Shirley**) You left Evelyn to meet the ratepayers?

Shirley (*to* **Greg**) Yes, I'd just popped back to collect the papers and stuff I was supposed to give to you.

Greg Evelyn, what happened?

Roy (*to* **Shirley**) I can't believe no one suspected a thing.

Shirley When I saw him earlier he didn't look well.

Roy Why didn't you say anything?

Shirley I did. I asked him if he was all right. He said he was.

Roy Why didn't you do something?

Shirley I'm not a doctor. You discharged him from hospital.

Roy Yes, but I don't have day-to-day contact.

Greg Shirley wasn't to know, Dr Freeman.

Roy Presumably, you do know that the words psychic and psychiatrist are not synonymous?

Greg He was no longer on a section. If he didn't want a doctor, then Shirley had no right to call one against his wishes.

Roy If someone has a heart attack, even if the last words they spoke were, 'If I have a heart attack, don't call the doctor!' you jolly well do because we don't practise euthanasia in this country yet.

Greg I think you've misconstrued what I was trying to say Dr Freeman. (*To* **Evelyn**.) Evelyn, what exactly happened?

Lil *comes back in with the tea.*

Eve Tell them.

Evelyn Shirley asked me to see those people. I met them in the hall. I showed them in here like you said. I didn't see him there. Not at first. Well, I did. But, I didn't expect – I didn't think anything was wrong. Well, I sort of did but I didn't want to make a fuss, cause alarm.

Lil You didn't want to make a fuss.

Eve I did. I did.

Evelyn I couldn't.

Nicola (*to* **Lil**) I'm surprised you find that hard to believe.

Lil (*to* **Nicola**) You didn't know him like I did. (*To* **Evelyn**.) How could you carry on like nothing had happened?

Evelyn I don't know.

Roy Why didn't you check to see if he was all right when you first saw him?

Evelyn I don't know.

Greg You don't know?

Shirley Evelyn wasn't to know, she'd only just arrived.

Greg It was unfortunate that you had to go out.

Shirley Even if I did get paid for it, I don't have the metaphysical capacity to be in two places at once.

Evelyn Shirley said he often had a sleep in the afternoons.

Lil You must know the difference between being dead and asleep.

Evelyn How?

Roy I don't believe this, one of my patients has died and I've not had a straight answer since I arrived.

Shirley We don't know! We knew he'd been mentally ill, but we had precious little knowledge about his physical health.

Roy My God, the whole world can see in, where are the curtains.

Lil We took them down for the painting. I was talking to Dave when I was mending them.

Roy Do you think they could go back ASAP. No not now. When we've gone will do. So you were the last person to have seen him, is that right?

Lil Yes, I was the last person not to notice anything. The last person to mend the curtains, clean the kitchen, prepare the meal, use the phone to let the Sparidae project know I couldn't make it this afternoon. I was the last person to have talked to him and I couldn't feel any worse than I do now for not realizing.

Greg I realize it's been upsetting for all of us. Dave was –

Lil You don't know him like I do.

Nicola He's dead.

Greg Let's put the brakes on. There was nothing any of us could have done.

Shirley It's my responsibility. I wasn't there and I should have been.

Eve While they stand and point and tell each other you're to blame, I am smashing my fist, splitting my skull. Inside my head someone is wielding an axe. I am smashing all the things in my father's house. Everything is splintering around me. Every stick of furniture lies useless and broken. I am crashing my way through the brickwork and plaster, the rendering and the mortar until nothing, nothing is left of my father's house but rubble and dust. And it goes on and on and it will never stop.

Roy So he was on his own. When Evelyn came in he'd died?

Evelyn Are you blaming me?

Roy No, of course not.

Evelyn You think I'm to blame though, don't you.

Roy No I don't.

Lil If anyone's got stick, it's me.

Greg No one's to blame. It's not a question of blame.

Evelyn You think it's all my fault.

Shirley No one's implied that Evelyn.

Roy Are you all right Evelyn?

Evelyn Is that a real question or is it, what's the word Lil, you're so much better with words than me?

Lil Rhetorical?

Evelyn Rhetorical.

Roy Of course it's a real question. You're imagining . . .

Evelyn Yes, yes, I know all about imagining that I'm not here, I'm somewhere else.

Greg Evelyn, I think you're in a state of shock. Do you feel cold?

Roy Here. (*Offers his coat.*) Put this around you.

Evelyn Don't touch me.

Roy Now, I think we should all calm down and drink our tea.

Evelyn We? You mean me. That I need a cup of tea. I don't want a cup of tea, as though a cup of tea will make me better. I don't even like tea. How will that calm me down? You – you stride in here, pointing the finger, attacking me . . .

Roy Evelyn I don't know what you're talking about.

Lil Evelyn, it's all right.

Nicola No, it isn't. Evelyn, would you like me to drive you home? (*Takes scissors.*) Come on. You'll have to tell me how to get there.

Lil Nicola? What about me?

They go.

Roy What the hell does she think she's up to? Just who does that wretched Nurse Cretsley think she is?

Lil Adams.

Shirley She's your daughter isn't she?

Lil Not so as you'd think I'd notice.

Roy She's asking for trouble. Evelyn's obviously very perturbed and she's no idea how to handle it.

Shirley I can't understand why she was so upset. She never even spoke to Dave. (*To* **Lil**.) There's no love lost between you?

Lil Something's lost – that's for sure. Probably the stuff between my ears.

Shirley I don't think so.

Lil Well I'm not laughing.

Roy (*sighs*) 'The troubled world is sighing now. Death is at the door. And many folks are dying now, who've never died before.'

Lil, **Shirley** *and* **Greg** *look at him.*

Shirley She doesn't speak to you?

Lil We don't see eye to eye.

Roy I'm so sorry. I don't know what made me say that. Some childhood rhyme popped into my head for no reason at all. (*Then.*) There's no point in going over the top. This sort of thing happens all the time. It leaves a place and we should fill it as soon as we can. Did you get the fire alarm business sorted out?

Shirley Yes, that's the stuff I wanted Greg to authorize.

Roy Good. (*To* **Greg**.) Can you get the ball rolling and bring Dawn on a visit?

Greg Will do.

Roy Right. We'd better be getting back.

Greg It was Nicola's car.

Roy That's the final straw.

Lil The 23 bus will take you most of the way there.

Scene Eight

Exodus

A supermarket.

Evelyn *is throwing groceries into a shopping trolley.* **Eve** *is cowering against the shelves watching her.* **Nicola** *stands in front of* **Evelyn**.

Evelyn You don't understand, I have to shop for him, it's my duty. He doesn't ask much, never has.

Eve *laughs.*

Nicola Evelyn.

Evelyn It's the least I can do.

Eve Stop it, stop it.

Nicola It doesn't have to be done now.

Evelyn Soonest done least mended.

Eve You don't have to behave like this.

Evelyn I do have to do it you see otherwise/

Eve No, you don't.

Evelyn They might have to send him away.

Nicola Evelyn. I would like us to go now. Evelyn?

Evelyn Yes?

Nicola There's no need.

Evelyn But the shopping?

Nicola Leave it. I'll drive you home.

Eve No please. Not home.

Evelyn Ummm.

Nicola I said let's go home.

Evelyn Can we just walk?

Nicola Er/

Evelyn There's something I want to tell you.

*They leave the supermarket. Open air. Early evening. They walk.
Silence.*

Scene Nine

Genesis

Nicola How are you feeling?

Evelyn Calmer. (*Then.*) Oh God, how am I ever going to face them again? (*She looks over her shoulder.*)

Nicola That doesn't matter now.

Evelyn I didn't want to go home.

Nicola It's all right.

Silence.

Evelyn Phillip might be there and if you have time I'd like to talk.

Nicola Fine.

Silence.

Evelyn Lil's your mother isn't she?

Nicola Only by birth.

Evelyn She told me you were a hairdresser.

Nicola I used to say I wanted to be one when I was small.

Evelyn She's never liked me. (*Pause.*) I don't like myself much.

Nicola Have you any children?

Evelyn A daughter. Still at school. Away at school. (*She looks behind her.*)

They cross the road and walk until they get to a bench on a piece of grass in the middle of a housing estate.

Evelyn *sits,* **Eve** *sits on one side of her,* **Nicola** *on the other.*

Evelyn This used to be an expanse of wasteland. Behind that block of flats there is the canal.

Nicola This estate must have been built about twenty years ago. Certainly council housing like this hasn't been built in the last ten years.

Evelyn People shouldn't be made to live like that.

Nicola No.

Evelyn There's something I want to tell you. Back there I felt an overwhelming urge to scream it in Roy Freeman's face. But something stopped me.

Nicola (*pause*) I'm listening.

Evelyn Now, I just want to go to sleep and not think about it.

Eve Just say it.

Evelyn It's about my father.

Eve It's about me.

Evelyn (*blurts out*) You see the first time it happened I thought it was my mistake. The bathroom. He came into the bathroom, which wasn't unusual in itself. He asked me for a cuddle, that wasn't unusual either but there was something in the way he touched me that made me feel uncomfortable. Even so, if it had never happened again I would have thought it was my mistake.

Nicola But it wasn't.

Evelyn No, you don't understand, he's such a well thought of man. Important, respected.

Eve What about me?

Nicola I believe you.

Evelyn Everyone admired him, being so busy and still managing to find time to spend with his children. He would take my brothers to cricket matches and he would make special time to do the things I wanted. I liked to go to the zoo. I'd been on a school trip there. I wasn't really interested in the animals. I found them boring but in a small corner was a wishing well. It seemed like magic to me.

Eve And?

Evelyn Actually, it was more of a small pond with a rockery around it and a little waterfall splashing onto a bed of coins. I was entranced by it and the first time we went together I took him straight over to see it. He seemed to understand. He said 'This'll be our secret'.

Eve There's more.

Evelyn But, on the way home he stopped the car and this time I knew it was not a mistake. (*Pause.*) From then on I would try and insist that I went to the cricket with my brothers. And my mother would chide me for being so ungrateful when I was lucky to have such a caring father. And I would walk around, lingering longer and longer, hoping that there wouldn't be enough time to stop the car and praying that this time would be different because I loved him and I wanted it to be all right.

Eve But it wasn't. It never has been.

Nicola I understand.

Evelyn Do you?

Nicola Yes.

Evelyn When he got wise to my time wasting, looking and looking into empty cages, pretending I was dying to see whatever creature it was that never appeared, he did it before. He stopped the car on the way to the zoo. Then I was supposed to walk round and enjoy myself. But, I would stop and look into the pond and refuse to move until it was time to go. He would grab my hand and squeeze his loose change into it and indicate that I could throw it in. And, I wanted to, but I couldn't. I held it so tightly I couldn't let go.

Eve I held it so tightly I couldn't let go.

Evelyn And the threats got worse. What would be done to me, to him, to my mother. And I wanted none of these things to happen. I just wanted it to stop.

Nicola And eventually it did?

Evelyn Yes.

Eve Just like it had never happened.

Evelyn *nods.*

Nicola You never told anyone?

Evelyn How could I?

Nicola What about your mother? Do you think she knew?

Eve No.

Evelyn No. I used to. But I don't any more.

Nicola What made you think she did?

Evelyn He did. Everything he did to me was carefully planned. At the time I thought she knew and didn't care because he planted that idea in my head.

Nicola How can you be sure?

Evelyn (*quietly*) I can't. She's not here to ask. She's dead. But I can remember in front of her and other people that mattered, he'd use certain words, say things that were significant to me but of course not to them. Only at the time I didn't realize. I thought they all knew and found it endearing.

Nicola How do you mean?

Eve *pulls her knees up to her chin and holds herself tightly.*

Evelyn Things like. (*Deep breath.*) He would make a big fuss making me wipe myself. He always carried a new hankie, which he would then throw away. He would give it to me and say 'wipe, wipe' in a forced jolly way and move his arms back and forth like windscreen wipers. Then in front of other people, if something got spilt, like a drink, he would give me his hankie and laugh and go 'wipe, wipe'. And they'd smile at my obedience.

Nicola There are ways of knowing, suspecting, however carefully they've covered up.

Evelyn Are there?

Nicola Without a child needing to find the words to say it.

Evelyn My mother warned me as conscientiously, as her mother had warned her, to beware of strange men. But strange men live in twilight worlds, haunt open spaces. They do not have homes, families, children. They are not the men you marry, depend on, build your whole life around. Because if they were, there would be the words to say, 'Don't be alone with your father – he's . . . he's . . .' (*She cannot finish the sentence. She looks at the ground.*)

Nicola It's over . . .

Eve I'm still hurting.

Evelyn Is it? I still feel so ashamed. If only I'd been able to stop it when it first started.

Nicola If he did that to your daughter would you blame her?

Evelyn Of course not.

Nicola Well.

Evelyn It's not that simple.

Nicola No.

Scene Ten

House built on sand

Evelyn's *father's house.*

Evelyn/Eve *enter the kitchen.* **Evelyn** *puts down the two bags of shopping she's carrying on the floor.* **George** *greets her smiling. He thrusts an envelope containing ten £10 notes in her hand.*

George Last time I saw you, you rushed off so suddenly I forgot to pay you for the shopping.

Evelyn (*looking in the envelope*) That's too much.

George Just a little pressie to say thank you – take it, what use is money to me at my age?

Eve (*moans*) Oh no, no.

George Would you like me to give you a hand with these? (*Lifting the bags and putting them down again.*)

Evelyn No, leave them. Sit down Dad I want to talk to you.

George (*pleased*) Right. I'll fill the kettle then shall I?

Evelyn No need. It's a long time 'til four o'clock.

George What's that?

Evelyn One of Roy Freeman's gems.

George (*filling the kettle all the same*) Oh, I saw him the other day. Nice chap. Did he tell you? Of course you rang while I was still there. Some poor blighter died in that home. It must have been terrible for you finding him like that.

Evelyn Yes it was.

Eve I've not come to talk about that.

Evelyn What did he want to see you about?

George (*sitting down*) He didn't. I bumped into him. It's a long story but I was asked to examine a little girl who was terminally ill.

Eve I feel cold. So cold.

Evelyn I've been thinking about my life.

George People usually do when someone they know dies.

Evelyn I didn't know him. Really.

George I can remember the first patient who died on me. I went through hell.

Evelyn Do you remember when I was young?

George Of course I do. You were what your grandmother always described as a bonny child.

Evelyn I wasn't very good at school.

George Well, in the fifties education wasn't considered very important for girls. A shame because of course it is.

Evelyn Do you remember taking me for days out?

George The cricket, yes. The boys wanted to move to Kennington so we could be near the Oval.

Eve He doesn't remember.

Evelyn No, me. Can you remember – taking me to the zoo?

George Well, of course, at my age, I can't remember every detail.

Eve You bastard. I can.

Evelyn You had a bloody season ticket.

George There's no need to be like that. Yes, yes I do, now you come to mention it, vaguely. You were very taken with all the money in that pond.

Evelyn I didn't like going.

George Yes, you did. Don't you remember that ghastly, ornamental rockery fascinated you.

Evelyn (*quietly.*) I remember screaming in the back of your car.

George Bonny you might have been but you could also be wilful and obstinate.

Eve Just tell him. Tell him.

Evelyn I remember being raped by you.

George (*shocked*) Evelyn! What on earth made you say a thing like that?

Evelyn You know what I'm talking about.

George I don't.

Evelyn What do you call it then?

George Call what?

Evelyn What you did to me.

George I don't know what you're talking about.

Evelyn (*angry*) You're not talking to someone who wasn't there. You're talking to me.

George (*unbelieving*) What is all this? Evelyn, for God's sake. Are you mad?

Eve (*questioning herself*) Who's mad? Who's mad?

George If you're going to carry on in this silly way, you can just go. (*He turns away and starts to put the shopping away.*)

Evelyn I know I can now. (*Spits out.*) 'Our secret.' Do you remember? Do you remember when I bought bolts for my bedroom door?

George Yes.

Evelyn And why do you think I did that?

George To stop anyone coming into your room.

Evelyn No, not anyone.

George Me.

Evelyn And why?

George To stop me going into your room.

Evelyn But I didn't find a way to stop you, I was too stupid.

Eve I was too frightened.

George It never happened.

Evelyn It did.

George Evey, let me.

Eve Make yourself say it.

George Just go, get out.

Evelyn I remember pleading with you at first. Then I fought with you but you were stronger. Then later I remember, can still remember, every grain, every pattern, every mark on that car seat while I wished myself away. It was as though I was standing outside the car looking in, looking down on another me that I despised.

George (*wanting her to stop*) Stop it!

Evelyn That's how it was.

Eve That's how it was.

George (*turns to face her*) It wasn't. You were special, vulnerable. I wanted to keep you to me. It was the only way I knew to show love. It wasn't talked about then. The boys, cricket matches and all that, that was different. I was closer to you.

Eve You fucking liar.

Evelyn Special?

George (*upset*) Oh Evelyn, you don't understand. I loved you. You mustn't think for one moment I didn't love you. I never wanted to hurt you. Really I didn't. I just wanted you to love me.

Evelyn You didn't love me. You bullied me, despised me. I was always hurting.

George I didn't know how to love. Nobody ever taught me.

Evelyn And that's what I learnt from you. I have never trusted anyone. I have existed, got by, doing what was expected of me, a hollow performance, almost convincing. I dare say Phillip, as you hinted, does have affairs. It never occurred to me I've been too busy defending myself against being betrayed.

George You know, now you're grown up, how men are. We're all weak and we're all strong. I didn't know about children. I wanted to be part of it. I didn't want to spoil it.

Evelyn You were a grown man.

George You don't know what it was like for me. I didn't even know myself what I was doing.

Eve Everything was planned down to the last detail.

Evelyn I don't believe it, any of it. You're lying.

George Evey, I'm an old man now please forgive me. You're all I've got. You, Phillip, Joanna.

Evelyn It's not our secret any more. I've told them. And I've written to Roy Freeman, as I will anyone else who might want a medical opinion of their daughter.

George How dare you? How dare you? You stupid bitch. Evey, it wasn't all like that. You're making it into something more than it was. You had everything.

Evelyn Bribery.

George They won't believe you. They'll think you're mad.

Evelyn I wonder why. But I'm not protecting you any more.

George (*explodes*) Revenge, that's what you want – all these years you've stored it up. Waited till your mother was out of the way. Now you want your own back, is that it?

Evelyn (*calmly*) There was a child who was abused by her Father for many years. It hurt. She was in pain and humiliated and eventually robbed of herself. No, Father, I don't want revenge. What could I possibly do to you that would undo what you've done to me? I've lived with it and I don't want to any longer. You can live with it. (**Eve** *turns and looks at* **Evelyn** *and slips away.*) And I won't forgive you because what you've done is unforgivable.

Eve *holds out a large bath towel towards* **Evelyn**. **Evelyn** *takes it and slowly starts to wipe her hands and face and neck, carefully, taking pleasure in it. She repeats the action with* **Eve**.

Scene Eleven

St Dymphna's

A week later.

Shirley *helps* **Lil** *put the mirror on the wall.*

Shirley This isn't in our job description.

Lil These days people either have work or they don't. Job descriptions got thrown out with free enterprise. At least Teddy will be pleased that the chair covers got dry cleaned.

Shirley What a weird bloke. He seemed more frightened of newspapers than the wrath of God.

Lil S'pose it's only human really.

Shirley Evelyn's resigned from the Management Committee. I couldn't persuade her to change her mind. Though I did try.

Lil Oh.

Shirley I thought you'd be pleased.

Lil I don't know what I am.

Shirley Lil, you know what you told me.

Lil Forget it, Shirley. We were all overwrought.

Nicola *comes in.*

Nicola The front door's wide open.

Shirley It's about to get a coat of anti-graffiti paint. Is this an official visit?

Nicola Only in so much as Dr Freeman sent me to collect his coat.

Shirley Oh. Yes. It's . . . (*She goes to get it.*)

Lil I know where it is. I'll get it. (*She goes.*)

Shirley Do you have time for a cup of coffee?

Nicola No, I'm sorry, I'm afraid I don't.

Shirley Then I wonder if you'd mind giving me a lift back to the hospital. I have to see Greg. Hopefully, we'll be ready for Dawn to move in at the beginning of the month.

Lil *comes in with the coat.*

Pause.

Shirley *takes it from her and goes to give it to* **Nicola**.

Nicola I thought you wanted a lift.

Shirley I do.

Nicola Well you can carry the coat then.

Shirley If we go out the back we can collect the file on the way. See you later Lil.

Shirley and **Nicola** *go.* **Lil** *starts to polish the mirror.*

Evelyn, *alone, comes in.* **Lil** *sees her in the mirror.*

Lil (*turns*) I thought you'd . . . Shirley said.

Evelyn I've come to take the picture back to the library.

Lil It's here. (*She gets it.*) Are you all right?

Evelyn (*taking the picture*) Thanks. No, but I will be.

Lil ⎫ I wanted

Evelyn ⎭ Are you

Lil Go on.

Evelyn Are you still frightened of flying?

Lil No. I never was. What I'm frightened of is crashing; sinking with the wreckage.

Evelyn So was I.

Scene Twelve

World without

Outside **Lil**'s *front door.* **Nicola** *hesitates before ringing the bell. She steps back as near to the balcony as she can, in case she decides to run.* **Lil** *opens the door, a book in her hand, her finger marking the page.*

Tony (*VO*) Who the hell is it?

Lil *looks behind her, then drops the book on the floor.*

Lil It's for me.

Steps over the threshold shutting the door behind her. The two women stand facing each other.